# LYLE'S GOLDEN COOKBOOK

# Cookbook

RECIPES WITH GOLDEN SYRUP
SUPPLIED AND TESTED BY
GOOD HOUSEKEEPING INSTITUTE

Published by Ebury Press
National Magazine House
72 Broadwick Street
London W1P 2BP

on behalf of The Home Economics Department of Tate & Lyle Refineries

First impression 1984

Edited by Nicole Foster
Designed by Roger Daniels
Photographs by James Jackson

Computerset by MFK Typesetting Ltd
Printed and bound in Italy by
New Interlitho s.p.a., Milan

*Cover photograph:* Profiteroles (page 55),
Moroccan Lemon Chicken (page 8),
Glazed Potatoes (page 37), Avocado Salad with
Orange Dressing (page 34) and Spicy Punch (page 111).

# CONTENTS

# INTRODUCTION

For the last 100 years Lyle's golden syrup has been produced in East London, and the famous green and gold can has become an essential feature in many kitchens, at home and abroad.

During this time countless tasty recipes have been developed which display the versatility of golden syrup. Here now is a selection of both traditional favourites and exciting new dishes – all of which are delicious!

---

### MEASURING LYLE'S GOLDEN SYRUP

15 ml (1 tbsp) = about 25 g (1 oz)
150 ml (¼ pint) = about 200 g (7 oz)
300 ml (½ pint) = about 400 g (14 oz)

**Using scales with weights or with slide mechanism**
Weigh the tin without the lid. From this weight, deduct the amount of syrup needed in the recipe. Adjust weights or slide an equivalent amount. Spoon out syrup from the tin until scales balance.

**Using pressure scales**
Weigh the tin without the lid. Deduct the amount of syrup needed in the recipe and note the resulting weight. Spoon out the syrup required, stopping when the scales indicate the latter weight.

---

### COOK'S TIPS

● Lyle's golden syrup will mix more easily if it is slightly warmed beforehand; it should not be refrigerated.

● If the syrup has been stored in a cool place, warm it slightly by standing the tin in hot water.

● Rinse measures and spoons in very hot water before use, then syrup can be scraped off cleanly without waste.

● For melting methods, weigh the saucepan first. Add the weight of syrup needed and then spoon syrup into the saucepan until the required weight is reached.

● For dripless pouring, rub the rim of the syrup tin with cooking oil before using.

● 5 ml (1 tsp) syrup added to tomato-based sauces and casseroles helps counteract the sharpness of tomatoes.

● Syrup can be used as a quick glaze for nuts when decorating cakes and biscuits.

An early poster

# MAIN DISHES

## Moroccan Lemon Chicken

*Illustrated on the jacket*

1 Lemon
60 ml (4 tbsp) Lyle's Golden Syrup
Pinch of Saffron
2.5 ml (½ level tsp) Mild Curry Powder
Pinch of Allspice
Salt and Freshly Ground Pepper
30 ml (2 tbsp) Vegetable Oil
6 Chicken Breasts, Skinned
200 ml (7 fl oz) Chicken Stock
Watercress Sprigs to Garnish

Halve the lemon lengthwise and cut into thin slices, discarding the pips. In a bowl, mix 30 ml (2 tbsp) syrup with the saffron, curry powder, allspice and seasoning. Add the lemon slices, cover the bowl and leave to marinate overnight.

Place the lemon with the marinade and 300 ml (½ pint) water in a saucepan. Cover and simmer for 1 hour, or until really tender. Heat the oil in a frying pan, add the remaining syrup and the chicken breasts, and fry over a moderate heat, turning frequently until a rich dark brown.

Add the lemon mixture and stock, bring to the boil, cover and simmer for 15–20 minutes, or until the chicken is tender. Adjust the seasoning, adding more syrup if necessary. Garnish with watercress before serving.

———— *SERVES 4* ————

# Syrup and Mustard Pork

1.4–1.8 kg (3–4 lb) Leg of Pork, Scored
75 ml (5 tbsp) Dijon Mustard
75 ml (5 tbsp) Lyle's Golden Syrup
30 ml (2 tbsp) Vegetable Oil
Salt and Freshly Ground Pepper
15 ml (1 level tbsp) Plain Flour
300 ml (½ pint) Chicken Stock
Few Drops of Gravy Browning

Remove the rind from the pork with a small sharp knife. Place the leg in a roasting tin lined with a piece of foil large enough to loosely wrap the whole joint. Combine the mustard, syrup and oil, and season with plenty of pepper. Smear the mixture all over the meat, and leave in a cool place overnight.

At cooking time, wrap the foil over the meat and roast in the oven at 180°C (350°F) mark 4 for 25 minutes per 450 g (1 lb) plus 25 minutes, or until the pork is tender. Open up the foil after 2 hours and baste the joint.

Meanwhile, cut the pork rind into fine strips from the fat side. Put in a tin, sprinkle with salt and cook alongside the joint for about 1½ hours until crisp. Serve hot with the pork.

Remove the pork from the foil and keep warm. Pour off nearly all the fat from the roasting tin. Place over a low heat and stir the flour into the meat juices. Cook for 1–2 minutes, then slowly blend in the stock. Bring to the boil, reduce heat and simmer for 5 minutes. Adjust seasoning, add a few drops of gravy browning and strain into a sauceboat.

*SERVES 4*

# Lamb with Orange Sauce

2 Large Breasts of Lean Lamb, Boned
75 g (3 oz) Fresh Breadcrumbs
2 Oranges
2.5 ml (½ level tsp) Dried Mint
1 Egg, Beaten
Salt and Freshly Ground Pepper
4 Medium Onions, Skinned
300 ml (½ pint) Chicken Stock
10 ml (2 level tsp) Cornflour
15 ml (1 tbsp) Lyle's Golden Syrup
10 ml (2 tsp) Worcestershire Sauce

Trim excess fat from the lamb. In a bowl, combine the breadcrumbs, grated rind from 1 orange (reserving the rest of the orange), mint, egg and seasoning. Spread the mixture over the meat, roll up, tie with string and place in an ovenproof casserole. Halve the onions crosswise, and arrange cut-side up round the lamb. Season with salt and pepper and add 60 ml (4 tbsp) stock. Cover the casserole and cook in the oven at 180°C (350°F) mark 4 for about 50 minutes, or until tender, uncovering for the last 20 minutes to brown.

Meanwhile, in a small saucepan, blend a little of the remaining stock with the cornflour, then add the rest with the golden syrup, Worcestershire sauce and the grated rind and juice from the second orange. Bring to the boil, stirring, and cook for 1–2 minutes. Season to taste. Divide the reserved orange into segments free of white pith.

Serve the lamb in thick slices with the orange sauce and reserved segments.

—————— *SERVES 4* ——————

# Chicken and Grape Salad

1.4 kg (3 lb) Oven Ready Chicken
1 Medium Onion, Skinned and Thickly Sliced
1 Large Carrot, Thickly Sliced
1 Bay Leaf
6 Peppercorns
2 Eggs
90 ml (6 tbsp) Lemon Juice
45 ml (3 tbsp) Lyle's Golden Syrup
150 ml (¼ pint) Whipping Cream
225 g (8 oz) White Grapes, Halved and Pipped
50 g (2 oz) Raisins
Salt and Freshly Ground Pepper
Lettuce Leaves and Paprika to Garnish

Place the chicken in a saucepan with the onion, carrot, bay leaf and pepper-corns. Cover with cold water, bring gently to the boil, cover, and poach for about 1¼ hours until tender. Cool in the stock, then divide the flesh into bite-size pieces. Reserve the stock for soups, sauces or freezing.

Beat the eggs with 60 ml (4 tbsp) lemon juice and the syrup. Cook in a double boiler or in a bowl over a pan of simmering water until thick. Cover with damp greaseproof paper and leave until cool.

Whip the cream lightly, and fold into the cold lemon mixture. Toss the prepared grapes in the remaining lemon juice and combine with the chicken, raisins and sauce. Season to taste. Serve garnished with lettuce leaves and a sprinkling of paprika.

———————— *SERVES 4–6* ————————

## Peanut Glazed Bacon

1.1 kg (2½ lb) Bacon Joint
1 Carrot, Peeled and Sliced
1 Onion, Skinned and Quartered
1 Bay Leaf
Grated Rind and Juice of 1 Lemon
60 ml (4 tbsp) Lyle's Golden Syrup
5 ml (1 tsp) Worcestershire Sauce
25 g (1 oz) Salted Peanuts, Chopped

Place the bacon in a large saucepan with the carrot, onion and bay leaf. Cover with cold water and bring slowly to the boil, skimming off any scum that forms. Cover and simmer for 50 minutes.

Remove the bacon, carefully cut off the rind and score the fat. In a bowl, combine the lemon rind, 10 ml (2 tsp) lemon juice, the golden syrup and Worcestershire sauce. Spread over the surface of the joint and press on the chopped peanuts. Place the joint in a roasting tin. Bake in the oven at 180°C (350°F) mark 4 for 25 minutes basting frequently. Raise the oven temperature to 220°C (425°F) mark 7, baste, and return to the oven for a further 15 minutes.

——————— *SERVES 6* ———————

## Barbecued Frankfurters with Beans

15 ml (1 tbsp) Vegetable Oil
1 Medium Onion, Skinned and Grated
20 ml (4 tsp) Prepared English Mustard
15 ml (1 tbsp) Lyle's Golden Syrup
45 ml (3 tbsp) Wine Vinegar
Two 447-g (15¾-oz) Cans Baked Beans
213-g (7½-oz) Packet Frankfurters
Salt and Freshly Ground Pepper
Tabasco Sauce

Heat the oil in a medium saucepan and add the onion. Cover the pan and cook over medium heat for about 5 minutes until the onion has softened. Stir in the mustard, syrup, vinegar and beans. Slice the frankfurters diagonally into 2-cm (¾-inch) pieces, and add to the bean mixture. Add salt, pepper and Tabasco sauce to taste. Cover and simmer gently for 10–15 minutes.

——————— *SERVES 4* ———————

# Chilli Con Carne

15 ml (1 tbsp) Fat or Vegetable Oil
700 g (1½ lb) Minced Beef
1 Large Onion, Skinned and Chopped
1 Medium Green Pepper, Seeded and Chopped
425-g (15-oz) Can Tomatoes
Salt and Freshly Ground Pepper
2.5 ml (½ level tsp) Chilli Powder or 30–45 ml (2–3 level tbsp)
Chilli Seasoning
15 ml (1 tbsp) Wine Vinegar
5 ml (1 tsp) Lyle's Golden Syrup
30 ml (2 tbsp) Tomato Purée
425-g (15-oz) Can Red Kidney Beans, Drained

Heat the fat or oil in a large frying pan and fry the mince until lightly browned, then add the onion and pepper and fry for 5 minutes, until soft. Stir in the tomatoes and season. Blend the chilli powder or seasoning with the vinegar, golden syrup and tomato purée, and add to the pan. Cover and simmer for 30–40 minutes, or until tender. Add the kidney beans 10 minutes before the cooking time is completed.

*SERVES 4*

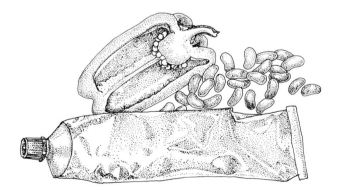

# Pot Roast Pork and Red Cabbage

450 g (1 lb) Red Cabbage, Shredded
45 ml (3 tbsp) Red Wine Vinegar
225 g (8 oz) Cooking Apples, Peeled, Cored and Sliced
15 ml (1 tbsp) Lyle's Golden Syrup
15 ml (1 level tbsp) Plain Flour
Salt and Freshly Ground Pepper
700 g (1½ lb) Boneless Pork Joint

Blanch the red cabbage in boiling water to which 15 ml (1 tbsp) vinegar has been added and drain well. Place the apple with the cabbage in an ovenproof casserole just wide enough to take the joint. Add the syrup, remaining vinegar, flour and seasoning and stir well together. Slash the fat side of the joint several times and season well. Place on top of the cabbage and cover the casserole.

Cook in the oven at 190°C (375°F) mark 5 for about 1¾ hours or until the pork is tender.

*———— SERVES 4 ————*

# Caramel Glazed Chicken

*Illustrated facing page 24*

4 Chicken Leg Quarters, 900 g (2 lb) Total Weight
50 g (2 oz) Butter or Margarine
Salt and Freshly Ground Pepper
90 ml (6 tbsp) Lyle's Golden Syrup
15 ml (1 tbsp) Lemon Juice
2 Garlic Cloves, Skinned and Crushed
Watercress Sprigs to Garnish

Dot chicken with the fat, sprinkle with salt and roast in the oven at 200°C (400°F) mark 6 for 30 minutes.

Place the syrup in a saucepan with 45 ml (3 tbsp) water and boil for 5–10 minutes to make a golden caramel. Allow to cool slightly. Stir in the lemon juice, 15 ml (1 tbsp) water and garlic, and season. Leave until cool and thickened to a coating consistency.

Pour fat from the chicken and spoon over the caramel glaze. Roast for a further 30 minutes, until well glazed and tender, basting frequently. Garnish with a few sprigs of watercress.

*———— SERVES 4 ————*

# Boston Beans

275 g (10 oz) Dried Haricot or Cannellini Beans, Soaked
Overnight
225 g (8 oz) Fat Salt Belly of Pork
15 ml (1 tbsp) Vegetable Oil
2 Medium Onions, Skinned and Chopped
5 ml (1 level tsp) Mustard Powder
15 ml (1 tbsp) Lyle's Black Treacle
15 ml (1 tbsp) Lyle's Golden Syrup
150 ml (¼ pint) Tomato Juice
30 ml (2 tbsp) Tomato Purée
300 ml (½ pint) Chicken Stock

Drain the beans and place in a saucepan of water. Bring to the boil and then boil for 25 minutes. Drain. Cut the pork into 2.5-cm (1-inch) cubes. Heat the oil in a flameproof casserole, and fry the onion for 5 minutes until soft. Off the heat, add the pork, beans and the remaining ingredients and stir well.

Bring up to the boil, then cook in the oven at 140°C (275°F) mark 1 for about 2½–3 hours, until the beans are tender and the sauce is the consistency of syrup. Stir from time to time to prevent sticking.

——————— *SERVES 4* ———————

# Sweet and Sour Meatballs

*Illustrated opposite*

50 g (2 oz) Butter or Margarine
1 Medium Onion, Skinned and Finely Chopped
450 g (1 lb) Minced Beef
50 g (2 oz) Fresh Brown Breadcrumbs
5 ml (1 tsp) Worcestershire Sauce
1 Egg
Salt and Freshly Ground Pepper
45 ml (3 tbsp) Vegetable Oil
1 Medium Green Pepper, Seeded and Roughly Chopped
1 Medium Red Pepper, Seeded and Roughly Chopped
30 ml (2 tbsp) Lyle's Golden Syrup
10 ml (2 tsp) Soy Sauce
30 ml (2 tbsp) Wine Vinegar
150 ml (¼ pint) Orange Juice
150 ml (¼ pint) Beef Stock
15 ml (1 level tbsp) Cornflour
Parsley to Garnish

Heat the fat in a saucepan, add the onion and cook for about 5 minutes until softened. Remove from the heat and stir in the mince, breadcrumbs, Worcestershire sauce and egg and season well. With damp hands, shape the mixture into twelve balls. Chill for 20 minutes.

Heat the oil in a flameproof casserole, and fry the meatballs until well browned. Remove with a slotted spoon. Add the peppers and sauté for 2 minutes. Stir in the soy sauce, vinegar, orange juice, stock and seasoning. Bring to the boil and replace the meatballs. Cover and cook in the oven at 180°C (350°F) mark 4 for about 45 minutes, or until tender, skimming if necessary.

Remove the meatballs from the pan and keep them warm in a serving dish. Mix the cornflour to a smooth paste with a little water; stir into the pan juices. Bring to the boil and cook, stirring for 2–3 minutes, then pour over the meatballs. Garnish with parsley and serve with noodles.

——————— *SERVES 4* ———————

*Glazed spare ribs; Sweet and sour meatballs.*

# Sweet-sour Rabbit with Prunes

*Illustrated opposite*

1 kg (2¼ lb) Prepared Rabbit, Jointed
300 ml (½ pint) Dry White Wine
175 g (6 oz) Onions, Skinned and Sliced
300 ml (½ pint) Chicken Stock
1 Bay Leaf
30 ml (2 tbsp) Lyle's Golden Syrup
Salt and Freshly Ground Pepper
8 Whole Prunes, Stoned
50 g (2 oz) Seedless Raisins
15 ml (1 tbsp) Malt Vinegar
10 ml (2 level tsp) Cornflour
Chopped Parsley and Fried Almonds to Garnish

Place the cleaned and jointed rabbit in a large bowl with the wine and onion and leave to marinate overnight. Next day, put the rabbit and marinade in a flameproof casserole and add the chicken stock, bay leaf, golden syrup and seasoning; bring to the boil. Add the prunes and raisins, cover the casserole tightly and cook in the oven at 170°C (325°F) mark 3 for about 1½ hours, until the rabbit is really tender and the prunes plump.

Remove the meat and keep warm in a serving dish. Blend the vinegar with the cornflour and add to the pan. Adjust the seasoning and boil for 1–2 minutes. Pour the thickened juices over the rabbit. Garnish with parsley and fried almonds before serving. Serve with baked potatoes.

——————— *SERVES 4* ———————

*Sweet-sour rabbit with prunes.*

# Apricot Stuffed Lamb

2 kg (4½ lb) Leg of Lamb, Boned
Plain Flour

──────── For the stuffing ────────
25 g (1 oz) Butter or Margarine
15 ml (1 tbsp) Lyle's Golden Syrup
1 Small Onion, Skinned and Grated
100 g (4 oz) Fresh White Breadcrumbs
2.5 ml (½ level tsp) Dried Thyme
1 Egg, Beaten
100 g (4 oz) Dried Apricots
Salt and Freshly Ground Pepper

──────── For the marinade ────────
1 Carrot, Peeled and Sliced
1 Onion, Skinned and Sliced
1 Bay Leaf
3 Parsley Stalks, Crushed
150 ml (¼ pint) Red Wine

Put the butter and golden syrup in a small saucepan, and melt over a low heat. Off the heat, add the onion, breadcrumbs, thyme and egg. Snip the apricots with scissors into the pan and season. Bind well together.

Wipe the lamb with a clean, damp cloth, trim off the excess fat from the top of the leg and spoon the stuffing into the cavity from which the bone was removed. Force the stuffing well down into the leg with the back of the spoon. Sew up with a trussing needle and fine string. Do not sew it too tightly, or the skin may split while the meat is roasting.

Place the meat in a large bowl. Add the marinade ingredients and leave in a cool place for about 6 hours, turning the meat occasionally in the juices. Remove from the marinade and weigh the stuffed joint. Strain the marinade and reserve.

Roast in the oven at 180°C (350°F) mark 4 for 25 minutes per 450 g (1 lb), or until the meat is tender. If the meat starts to over-brown, cover it with foil. Remove the string and place the joint on a serving dish. Keep hot. Pour off the fat from the roasting tin and stir a little flour into the juices. Cook on top of the stove for a few minutes. Add 30–45 ml (2–3 tbsp) of the strained marinade and a little water. Adjust seasoning. Bring to the boil, stirring, and simmer for a further 5 minutes. Serve the gravy separately.

──────── SERVES 6–8 ────────

# Barbecued Drumsticks

50 g (2 oz) Butter or Margarine
30 ml (2 tbsp) Lyle's Golden Syrup
1 Medium Onion, Skinned and Chopped
8 Chicken Drumsticks, Skinned
150 ml (¼ pint) Chicken Stock
30 ml (2 tbsp) Tomato Purée
30 ml (2 tbsp) Worcestershire Sauce
5 ml (1 level tsp) Tate & Lyle Demerara Sugar
5 ml (1 tsp) Wine Vinegar
Salt and Freshly Ground Pepper
227-g (8-oz) Can Tomatoes
15 g (½ oz) Sultanas

Heat the fat and syrup in a frying pan. Add the onion and fry for 2–3 minutes until soft. Add the drumsticks and fry for about 10 minutes, until well browned. Pour over the stock and cook for a further 10 minutes, until the liquid is reduced and thickened.

Add all the remaining ingredients. Bring to the boil, then simmer for a further 10 minutes, or until the chicken is tender.

Arrange the drumsticks on a warm serving dish and pour over the sauce.

*SERVES 4*

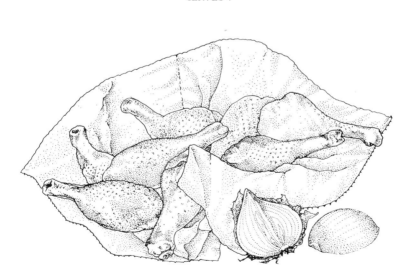

# ORIENTAL LAMB

900 g (2 lb) LAMB SHOULDER, BONED
15 ml (1 TBSP) VEGETABLE OIL
450 g (1 lb) WHITE CABBAGE, TRIMMED AND SHREDDED
175 g (6 oz) CARROT, PEELED AND FINELY SLICED
1 SMALL GREEN PEPPER, SEEDED AND CHOPPED
1 MEDIUM ONION, SKINNED AND THINLY SLICED
30 ml (2 TBSP) SOY SAUCE
15 ml (1 TBSP) WORCESTERSHIRE SAUCE
30 ml (2 TBSP) WINE VINEGAR
30 ml (2 TBSP) LYLE'S GOLDEN SYRUP
600 ml (1 PINT) CHICKEN STOCK
5 ml (1 LEVEL TSP) DRIED ROSEMARY
SALT AND FRESHLY GROUND PEPPER
1 CANNED PIMENTO CAP, THINLY SLICED
25 g (1 oz) NOODLES

Trim the lamb of excess fat and cut into 2.5-cm (1-inch) cubes. Heat the oil in a flameproof casserole, add the lamb and brown, turning occasionally. Stir in the cabbage, carrot, pepper and onion and cook gently for 5 minutes.

Meanwhile, in a bowl, mix the soy sauce, Worcestershire sauce, vinegar, syrup and stock together, pour over the lamb mixture, sprinkle in the rosemary and season well. Cover and simmer on top of the cooker, stirring occasionally, for about 50 minutes, or until tender. Add the pimento and noodles to the lamb, stirring well to mix, and continue to cook gently for a further 15 minutes until the noodles are just cooked.

*SERVES 4*

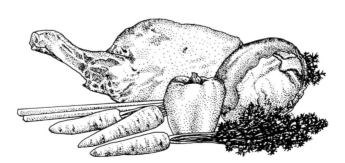

# Duck with Apricots

1.8–2.6 kg (4–6 lb) Oven Ready Duck
100 g (4 oz) Dried Apricots
Grated Rind and Juice of 1 Orange
1 Onion, Skinned and Finely Chopped
40 g (1½ oz) Plain Flour
450 ml (¾ pint) Chicken Stock
30 ml (2 tbsp) Lyle's Golden Syrup
Salt and Freshly Ground Pepper
425-g (15-oz) Can Apricot Halves
60 ml (4 tbsp) Brandy (Optional)
25 g (1 oz) Walnuts, Chopped, to Garnish

Place the duck in a roasting tin and roast in the oven at 200°C (400°F) mark 6 for 15 minutes per 450 g (1 lb), plus 15 minutes, or until tender. Meanwhile, place the dried apricots and orange juice and rind in a saucepan with 150 ml (¼ pint) water. Gently stew for 20 minutes until soft. Rub through a sieve or purée in a blender.

Remove the cooked duck from the roasting tin, joint it and place the pieces in a casserole. Drain excess fat from the tin, then fry the onion in the tin until coloured. Add the flour and continue cooking, stirring, for 3 minutes. Gradually add the stock, apricot purée and syrup. Boil for 2–3 minutes stirring. Season to taste and pour over the duck.

Heat the apricot halves with their juice and the brandy (if used) in a saucepan, drain and arrange over the duck. Garnish with chopped walnuts.

*SERVES 4*

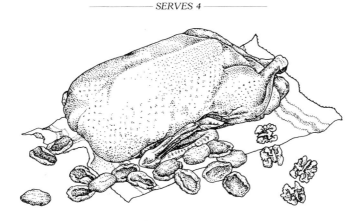

# STIR-FRIED PORK AND VEGETABLES

450 g (1 lb) MINCED PORK
1.25 ml (¼ LEVEL TSP) GROUND CORIANDER
SALT AND FRESHLY GROUND PEPPER
30 ml (2 TBSP) VEGETABLE OIL
2 MEDIUM ONIONS, SKINNED AND FINELY SLICED
350 g (12 oz) CABBAGE, FINELY SLICED
125 g (4 oz) BEANSPROUTS
15 ml (1 LEVEL TBSP) CORNFLOUR
10 ml (2 TSP) SOY SAUCE
30 ml (2 TBSP) LYLE'S GOLDEN SYRUP
150 ml (¼ PINT) CHICKEN STOCK
227-g (8-oz) CAN PINEAPPLE CHUNKS IN JUICE

Mix the pork with the coriander and season well. Shape into sixteen small cork shapes. Heat the oil in a large frying pan and brown the pork well. Stir in the onion, cabbage and beansprouts and cook for a further 5–7 minutes, stirring all the time, until the vegetables are just tender.

Mix the cornflour to a smooth paste with a little water, then add the soy sauce, golden syrup and stock. Stir the sauce mixture into the pan with the pineapple chunks and juice. Bring to the boil and simmer until thickened. Taste and adjust seasoning.

*SERVES 4*

# Sweet and Sour Lamb

1.4 kg (3 lb) Shoulder of Lamb, Boned
30 ml (2 tbsp) Vegetable oil
2 Medium Onions, Skinned and Sliced
5 ml (1 level tsp) Ground Ginger
45 ml (3 level tbsp) Plain Flour
450 ml (¾ pint) Chicken Stock
300 ml (½ pint) Dry Cider
30 ml (2 tbsp) Soy Sauce
15 ml (1 tbsp) Worcestershire Sauce
45 ml (3 tbsp) Lyle's Golden Syrup
45 ml (3 tbsp) Wine Vinegar
225-g (8-oz) Can Pineapple Chunks in Natural Juice
Salt and Freshly Ground Pepper
125 g (4 oz) Small Pasta Shells
1 Large Green Pepper, Seeded and Cut into Strips
Chopped Parsley to Garnish

Cut the lamb into 2.5-cm (1-inch) cubes, discarding excess fat. Heat the oil in a large flameproof casserole. Fry the lamb, a little at a time, until well browned. Remove from the pan and add the onion, ground ginger and flour. Fry gently for 3 minutes. Stir in the stock, cider, soy sauce, Worcestershire sauce, syrup and vinegar with the strained pineapple juice, seasoning and meat.

Bring to the boil, cover and cook in the oven at 180°C (350°F) mark 4 for 1½ hours. Add the pineapple, pasta and green pepper, re-cover and cook for a further 30 minutes, or until the meat is tender and the pasta is just cooked. Adjust seasoning to taste and garnish with parsley.

VARIATIONS

1. Replace the lamb with 1.4 kg (3 lb) loin or shoulder of pork, boned and cut into cubes.

2. Replace the pasta with 225 g (8 oz) potatoes, diced and cooked.

3. Replace the green pepper with 100 g (4 oz) mushrooms, sliced.

——————— *SERVES 4* ———————

## Barbecued Pork Chops

Salt and Freshly Ground Pepper
4 Large Pork Chump Chops, Trimmed of Fat
45 ml (3 tbsp) Lyle's Golden Syrup
30 ml (2 tbsp) Soy Sauce
45 ml (3 tbsp) Tomato Purée
1 Garlic Clove, Skinned and Crushed
2.5 ml (½ level tsp) Mustard Powder
Juice of 1 Large Orange
Juice of ½ a Small Lemon
15 ml (1 tbsp) White Wine Vinegar
15 ml (1 tbsp) Vegetable Oil
1 Small Onion, Skinned and Chopped

Season the chops well. In a bowl, mix together the golden syrup, soy sauce, tomato purée, crushed garlic, mustard, fruit juices and vinegar. Heat the oil in a frying pan and fry the chops quickly on both sides until browned. Remove them from the pan, drain and place in a shallow casserole together with the sauce mixture and the onion. Cover, and cook in the oven at 180°C (350°F) mark 4 for 30–40 minutes until the chops are tender. Serve with rice.

*————— SERVES 4 —————*

## Barbecued Turkey Burgers

*Illustrated opposite*

5 ml (1 level tsp) Mustard Powder
5 ml (1 tsp) Soy Sauce
30 ml (2 tbsp) Lyle's Golden Syrup
90 ml (6 tbsp) Tomato Ketchup
1 Small Onion, Skinned and Grated
4 Turkey Burgers

In a bowl, combine the mustard, soy sauce, syrup, ketchup and onion. Place the turkey burgers in a grill pan without the grid and spoon over the barbecue sauce. Grill for 7 minutes on each side or until cooked right through, basting often with the barbecue sauce. Serve in buttered baps, on a bed of shredded lettuce with any remaining sauce spooned over.

*————— SERVES 4 —————*

*Barbecued turkey burgers; Caramel glazed chicken.*
*Overleaf: Glazed bacon with herb stuffed apples. Cassoulet.*

# HADDOCK CURRY

*Illustrated opposite*

450 g (1 lb) FRESH HADDOCK FILLET
45 ml (3 TBSP) VEGETABLE OIL
1 LARGE ONION, SKINNED AND SLICED
1 GARLIC CLOVE, SKINNED AND CRUSHED
25 g (1 oz) DESICCATED COCONUT
15 ml (1 LEVEL TBSP) PLAIN FLOUR
5 ml (1 LEVEL TSP) GROUND CORIANDER
2.5 ml (½ LEVEL TSP) GROUND TURMERIC
1.25 ml (¼ LEVEL TSP) GROUND GINGER
150 ml (¼ PINT) FISH STOCK
15 ml (1 TBSP) LYLE'S GOLDEN SYRUP
25 g (1 oz) PEANUTS
100 g (4 oz) PEELED PRAWNS
SALT AND FRESHLY GROUND PEPPER
CHOPPED PARSLEY AND TOASTED COCONUT TO GARNISH

Skin the haddock and cut into 2.5-cm (1-inch) chunks. Heat the oil in a large frying pan and fry the onion and garlic for about 10 minutes, until browned. In a bowl, mix together the coconut, flour, coriander, turmeric and ginger. Add the haddock pieces and toss all together.

Add to the pan and fry gently until golden, stirring occasionally. Pour in the stock and syrup, bring to the boil and add the peanuts, prawns and seasoning. Cover and simmer for 5–10 minutes, or until the fish is tender. Adjust the seasoning and garnish with parsley and coconut. Serve with brown rice.

——— *SERVES 4* ———

*Haddock curry.*

# Peach Glazed Chicken Legs

50 g (2 oz) Brown Rice
15 ml (1 level tbsp) Ground Turmeric
Salt and Freshly Ground Pepper
50 g (2 oz) Butter or Margarine
125 g (4 oz) Spring Onions, Trimmed and Finely Chopped
25 g (1 oz) Brazil Nuts, Finely Chopped
2.5 ml (½ level tsp) Ground Ginger
411-g (14½-oz) Can Peach Halves
4 Chicken Legs, About 1 kg (2.2 lb) Total Weight
15 ml (1 tbsp) Lyle's Golden Syrup
5 ml (1 level tsp) Cornflour
15 ml (1 tbsp) Malt Vinegar

Cook the brown rice with the turmeric in a saucepan of boiling salted water for about 45 minutes. Drain well. Heat 25 g (1 oz) fat in a frying pan and lightly fry the spring onion and nuts with the ginger for 2–3 minutes. Off the heat, stir in the cooked rice and one chopped peach half – reserve the peach juices. Season and leave until cool.

Cut and ease the bones out of the chicken legs, keeping the skin and flesh as intact as possible. Spoon a little of the rice stuffing into each chicken leg. Carefully fold over to enclose the stuffing, and sew up neatly.

In a blender, liquidise the remaining peaches with half the reserved juice, the golden syrup, cornflour and vinegar. Place in a small saucepan and boil, stirring all the time, until reduced by half.

Melt the remaining fat in a shallow 1.1-litre (2-pint) flameproof casserole and brown the chicken parcels. Pour over the peach sauce. Cook in the oven at 200°C (400°F) mark 6 for about 40 minutes, or until tender. Skim before serving.

*SERVES 4*

VARIATIONS
1. Replace the peach halves with apricot halves.
2. Replace the ground ginger with 2.5 ml (½ level tsp) curry powder.

# Turkey Escalopes in Curry Sauce

*Illustrated facing page 32*

4 Thin Turkey Escalopes or 450 g (1 lb) Turkey Fillet, Cut into
4 Pieces
Salt and Freshly Ground Pepper
225 g (8 oz) Pork Sausagemeat or Sausages
30 ml (2 tbsp) Mango Chutney
30 ml (2 tbsp) Vegetable Oil
2 Large Onions, Skinned and Sliced
15 ml (1 level tbsp) Ground Cumin
45 ml (3 level tbsp) Plain Flour
45 ml (3 level tbsp) Desiccated Coconut
450 ml (¾ pint) Chicken Stock
15 ml (1 tbsp) Lyle's Golden Syrup
10 ml (2 tsp) Lemon Juice
Coriander to Garnish

B at out the escalopes or fillet between sheets of damp greaseproof paper until thin. Season well. Mix the sausagemeat (or skinned sausages) with 15 ml (1 tbsp) chutney and season. Divide between the escalopes. Roll up, and secure with wooden cocktail sticks.

Heat the oil in a shallow flameproof casserole and quickly brown the rolled escalopes. Remove with a fish slice. Add the onion, cumin, flour and coconut to the casserole, and fry for 2–3 minutes. Stir in the remaining ingredients and season. Bring to the boil, and replace the turkey escalopes in a single layer.

Cover and cook in the oven at 150°C (300°F) mark 2 for 1½ hours, or until turkey is tender. Skim and serve on a bed of rice. Garnish with coriander leaves.

——— *SERVES 4* ———

# Glazed Spare Ribs

*Illustrated facing page 16*

1.4 kg (3 lb) American Spare Ribs of Pork
90 ml (6 tbsp) Lyle's Golden Syrup
60 ml (4 tbsp) Lemon Juice
150 ml (¼ pint) Dry Cider
60 ml (4 tbsp) Soy Sauce
8 Black Peppercorns
2.5 ml (½ level tsp) Salt
15 ml (1 level tbsp) Arrowroot
2 Small Grapefruit, Peeled and Segmented
Chopped Parsley to Garnish

Divide the pork into individual ribs and trim off excess fat. Place in a shallow dish. In a small saucepan, heat the syrup, lemon juice, cider, soy sauce, peppercorns and salt until well blended. Take off the heat, leave until cool, then pour over the ribs, cover and marinate overnight in the refrigerator.

Place meat and marinade in an ovenproof dish, cover and cook in the oven at 190°C (375°F) mark 5 for 2 hours, or until the meat is tender, basting frequently. Arrange the spare ribs on a serving dish and keep warm. Strain the marinade into a small saucepan. Blend the arrowroot to a smooth paste with 45 ml (3 tbsp) water. Add to the marinade in the pan and bring to the boil, stirring until thickened. Add the grapefruit to the sauce, adjust seasoning to taste, and spoon over the spare ribs. Garnish with chopped parsley.

--------- *SERVES 4* ---------

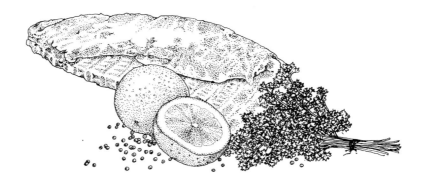

# Cassoulet

*Illustrated between pages 24 and 25*

350 g (12 oz) Dried Haricot Beans, Soaked Overnight
225 g (8 oz) Rindless Streaky Bacon, Finely Chopped
2 Large Garlic Cloves, Skinned and Finely Chopped
2 Medium Onions, Skinned and Finely Chopped
175 g (6 oz) Boned Neck of Lamb
225 g (8 oz) Garlic Sausage
50 g (2 oz) Butter or Margarine
6–8 Chicken Thighs or Drumsticks, about 700 g (1½ lb) Total Weight
450 g (1 lb) Tomatoes, Skinned and Quartered
2 Sticks of Celery, Washed, Trimmed and Finely Sliced
150 ml (¼ pint) Red Wine
400 ml (¾ pint) Chicken Stock
15 ml (1 tbsp) Lyle's Golden Syrup
30 ml (2 tbsp) Tomato Purée
10 ml (2 tsp) Dijon Mustard
2 Bay Leaves
Salt and Freshly Ground Pepper

Drain the beans, then place in a saucepan of water and boil for 30 minutes. Drain. Put the bacon in a frying pan and heat until the fat runs. Add the garlic and onion and fry for 10 minutes, or until well browned. Place in a large ovenproof dish with the beans.

Cut the lamb and sausage into 2.5-cm (1-inch) cubes. Heat the fat in the frying pan and fry the chicken and lamb until lightly browned. Place in the ovenproof dish with the sausage, tomatoes, celery, wine, stock, syrup, tomato purée, mustard, bay leaves and seasoning. Stir well.

Cover the dish and cook in the oven at 170°C (325°F) mark 3 for about 3 hours, or until beans and meat are tender. Stir from time to time to prevent sticking. Serve with French bread.

### VARIATION

For a traditional crusty topping sprinkle on 50 g (2 oz) breadcrumbs before cooking. Halfway through cooking time, press the crust down well and sprinkle on a further 50 g (2 oz) breadcrumbs.

——————— *SERVES 6–8* ———————

# Marinated Beef Salad

225 g (8 oz) Bean Sprouts
350 g (12 oz) Cooked Medium Rare Roast Beef
1 Medium Onion, Skinned and Thinly Sliced
125 g (4 oz) Green Pepper, Seeded
125 g (4 oz) Celery, Trimmed
175 g (6 oz) Carrot, Peeled
60 ml (4 tbsp) Sherry
30 ml (2 tbsp) Soy Sauce
15 ml (1 tbsp) Red Wine Vinegar
15 ml (1 tbsp) Lyle's Golden Syrup
Salt and Freshly Ground Pepper
Watercress Sprigs to Garnish

Wash the bean sprouts and drain thoroughly. Shred the beef and combine with the bean sprouts and onion. Finely slice the green pepper, celery and carrot and add to the beef mixture.

Combine the sherry, soy sauce, vinegar and syrup in a bowl and stir well until the syrup blends in. Pour this dressing over the beef and vegetables, add plenty of seasoning and stir well. Cover and leave in the refrigerator overnight.

To serve, toss the salad and turn on to a serving dish. Garnish with watercress sprigs.

### VARIATIONS

1. Replace the beef with 350 g (12 oz) cooked lean pork or the same quantity of cooked chicken.

2. Replace the bean sprouts with a 432-g (15¼-oz) can pineapple cubes, drained.

3. Sprinkle over 50 g (2 oz) cashew nuts or 15 ml (1 level tbsp) sesame seeds just before serving.

4. Replace the beef and carrot with 450 g (1 lb) peeled prawns and ½ a cucumber, cut into 2.5-cm (1-inch) strips.

*SERVES 4*

# Glazed Bacon with Herb Stuffed Apples

*Illustrated between pages 24 and 25*

1.8 kg (4 lb) Joint of Bacon, Soaked for 2 Hours
6 Small Cooking Apples, Cored
Whole Cloves
60 ml (4 tbsp) Lyle's Golden Syrup
Sage Sprigs to Garnish

——— *For the stuffing* ———
100 g (4 oz) Dried Breadcrumbs
1 Medium Onion, Skinned and Chopped
2 Sticks of Celery, Washed, Trimmed and Chopped
5 ml (1 level tsp) Dried Sage
30 ml (2 tbsp) Chopped Parsley
Salt and Freshly Ground Pepper
1 Egg, Beaten

Place the bacon joint in a large saucepan, cover with water and bring to the boil. Remove any scum from the water, cover and simmer gently for 1 hour. Drain, then place the bacon in a roasting tin. Cover with foil and bake in the oven at 180°C (350°F) mark 4 for 35 minutes.

For the stuffing, mix together in a bowl the stuffing ingredients with enough egg to bind. Score the apples around the centre and fill with the stuffing. Remove the skin from the bacon and score the fat with a knife. Stud with cloves and brush over the golden syrup.

Place the stuffed apples around the bacon and continue cooking for 30 minutes, or until the bacon is tender. Garnish with sage and serve.

——— *SERVES 6–8* ———

# VEGETABLES AND SALADS

### Barbecued Baked Beans

*Illustrated facing page 33*

1.1 litres (2 pints) Tomato Juice
1 Large Onion, Skinned and Chopped
60 ml (4 tbsp) Cider Vinegar
15 ml (1 tbsp) Worcestershire Sauce
15 ml (1 level tbsp) Mustard Powder
15 ml (1 tbsp) Lyle's Golden Syrup
Salt and Freshly Ground Pepper
5 ml (1 level tsp) Paprika
Two 410-g (14¼-oz) Cans White Haricot Beans, Drained

Put all the ingredients, except the beans, in a large saucepan. Bring to the boil and cook rapidly until reduced by half, stirring from time to time. Leave to cool, then rub through a sieve or purée in a blender until smooth. Return to the pan, add the beans and simmer for 10 minutes.

———— *SERVES 6* ————

*Turkey escalopes in curry sauce.*

# Potato, Carrot and Onion Bourguignonne

*Illustrated opposite*

25 g (1 oz) Butter or Margarine
15 ml (1 tbsp) Vegetable Oil
5 ml (1 tsp) Lyle's Golden Syrup
225 g (8 oz) Carrots, Peeled and Sliced
225 g (8 oz) Small Onions, Skinned
450 g (1 lb) Small New Potatoes, Scrubbed and Halved
125 g (4 oz) Button Mushrooms, Wiped
15 ml (1 level tbsp) Plain Flour
150 ml (¼ pint) Red Wine
10 ml (2 tsp) Tomato Purée
150 ml (¼ pint) Beef Stock
1 Bay Leaf
Salt and Freshly Ground Pepper
Parsley to Garnish

Heat the fat and oil together in a flameproof casserole. Add the syrup, carrots, onions and potatoes, and cook, stirring, until the vegetables begin to colour. Add the mushrooms and cook for a further minute. Stir in the flour, scraping any sediment from the bottom of the pan. Add the red wine, tomato purée, stock, bay leaf and seasoning and stir to mix.

Cover tightly and cook in the oven at 190°C (375°F) mark 5 for about 1 hour until tender. Before serving, remove the bay leaf and check the seasoning. Garnish with parsley.

———— SERVES 4 ————

*Potato, carrot and onion bourguignonne; Barbecued baked beans.*

# Avocado Salad with Orange Dressing

*Illustrated on the jacket and between pages 40 and 41*

150 ml (¼ pint) Vegetable Oil
60 ml (4 tbsp) Orange Juice
30 ml (2 tbsp) Lemon Juice
15 ml (1 tbsp) Lyle's Golden Syrup
Salt and Freshly Ground Pepper
½ Small Cucumber, Sliced
4 Sticks of Celery, Washed, Trimmed and Sliced
2 Ripe Avocados, Peeled, Stoned and Sliced
1 Head of Chicory, Trimmed and Washed
Shredded Orange Rind to Garnish

Whisk the oil, fruit juices, golden syrup and seasoning together and toss the cucumber, celery and avocado in the dressing. Arrange the chicory leaves in a serving dish and pile the salad on top. Sprinkle with the orange rind and serve immediately with cold meats or cheese.

———————— *SERVES 4* ————————

# Endive, Orange and Walnut Salad

*Illustrated between pages 40 and 41*

1 Endive
3 Oranges
25 g (1 oz) Walnut Pieces
5 ml (1 tsp) Lyle's Golden Syrup
142-ml (5-fl oz) Carton Soured Cream
30 ml (2 tbsp) Lemon Juice
Salt and Freshly Ground Pepper

Pull the endive apart, wash and dry thoroughly. Tear into pieces and place in a salad bowl. Remove the skin and all pith from 2 oranges and divide into segments. Add to the endive with the walnuts. Cover and keep refrigerated.

Grate the rind and squeeze the juice of the remaining orange. Just before serving combine with the golden syrup and soured cream and stir in the lemon juice. Season to taste. Spoon the completed dressing over the endive and then toss the mixture lightly.

———————— *SERVES 4–6* ————————

# Vegetable Casserole

40 g (1½ oz) Butter or Margarine
1 Onion, Skinned and Sliced
1 Small Green Pepper, Seeded and Sliced
450 g (1 lb) Potatoes, Peeled and Diced
1 Garlic Clove, Skinned and Crushed
5 ml (1 level tsp) Ground Coriander
5 ml (1 level tsp) Ground Cumin
40 g (1½ oz) Plain Flour
300 ml (½ pint) Chicken or Vegetable Stock
5 ml (1 tsp) Lyle's Golden Syrup
400-g (14-oz) Can Tomatoes
30 ml (2 tbsp) Tomato Purée
Salt and Freshly Ground Pepper
3 Courgettes, Trimmed, Washed and Sliced

Melt the fat in a saucepan and add the onion, pepper, potatoes, garlic and spices. Sauté for about 5 minutes. Stir in the flour and cook for 2 minutes. Gradually stir in the stock, syrup, tomatoes with juice and the tomato purée and bring to the boil to thicken, then season well. Cover and simmer gently for 20 minutes. Add the courgettes and continue cooking for 10 minutes until all the vegetables are tender.

*———— SERVES 4 ————*

# Vichy Carrots

450 g (1 lb) New Carrots, Trimmed and Scrubbed
25 g (1 oz) Butter or Margarine
Salt and Freshly Ground Pepper
15 ml (1 tbsp) Lyle's Golden Syrup
Parsley to Garnish

Place the carrots in a saucepan with 450 ml (¾ pint) water, half the fat, a pinch of salt and the syrup. Bring to the boil and cook uncovered over a low heat, shaking occasionally towards the end, for about 45 minutes, until all the liquid has evaporated. Add the remaining fat and some pepper and toss the carrots until glazed. Turn into a heated serving dish and garnish with parsley.

*———— SERVES 4 ————*

# Mushroom, Cucumber and Coriander Salad

*Illustrated facing page 41*

450 g (1 lb) Button Mushrooms, Sliced
120 ml (8 tbsp) Sunflower Oil
75 ml (5 tbsp) White Wine Vinegar
5 ml (1 tsp) Lyle's Golden Syrup
10 ml (2 level tsp) Ground or Finely Chopped Fresh Coriander
Salt and Freshly Ground Pepper
1 Large Cucumber
Chopped Coriander to Garnish

Place the mushrooms in a large bowl. Whisk together the oil, vinegar, syrup and coriander with salt and pepper to taste. Pour over the mushrooms and leave to marinate for about 30 minutes. Thinly slice the cucumber, cover and set aside. Just before serving, drain off any liquid from the cucumber and fold half the cucumber carefully through the mushrooms. Adjust the seasoning if necessary. Garnish with the rest of the cucumber and chopped coriander.

———— *SERVES 4* ————

# Mexican Beans

432-g (15¼-oz) Can Red Kidney Beans, Drained
60 ml (4 tbsp) Vegetable Oil
30 ml (2 tbsp) Malt Vinegar
Pinch of Chilli Powder
2.5 ml (½ tsp) French Mustard
15 ml (1 tbsp) Lyle's Golden Syrup
Salt and Freshly Ground Pepper
4 Sticks of Celery, Washed, Trimmed and Chopped
25 g (1 oz) Gherkins, Chopped
1 Small Onion, Skinned and Finely Chopped
1 Lettuce, Washed
A Few Celery Leaves to Garnish

Place the beans in a mixing bowl. Whisk or shake together the oil, vinegar, chilli powder, mustard, syrup, salt and pepper. Pour over the beans and toss together. Add the celery, gherkins and onion. Arrange the lettuce in a serving bowl and pile the bean mixture on top, spooning over any remaining dressing. Garnish with celery leaves.

———— *SERVES 4* ————

## GLAZED POTATOES

*Illustrated on the jacket*

700 g (1½ lb) NEW POTATOES, SCRUBBED OR SCRAPED
50 g (2 oz) BUTTER
30 ml (2 TBSP) LYLE'S GOLDEN SYRUP
20 ml (4 LEVEL TSP) TATE & LYLE LIGHT BROWN SOFT SUGAR
SALT AND FRESHLY GROUND PEPPER
CHOPPED PARSLEY TO GARNISH

Put the potatoes in a saucepan of salted water, bring to the boil and cook for 10–15 minutes until just cooked but still firm. Drain well. In the same cleaned pan, heat the butter, syrup, sugar and seasoning together. Add the potatoes and continue cooking, stirring until the potatoes are evenly coated. Serve garnished with parsley.

——————— *SERVES 4* ———————

## TURNIP AND WATERCRESS SALAD

*Illustrated between pages 40 and 41*

350 g (12 oz) TURNIPS, PEELED
1 BUNCH OF WATERCRESS, TRIMMED AND WASHED
150 ml (5 oz) NATURAL YOGURT
5 ml (1 TSP) LYLE'S GOLDEN SYRUP
5 ml (1 LEVEL TSP) MUSTARD POWDER
15 ml (1 LEVEL TBSP) GRATED HORSERADISH

Finely grate the turnips. Reserve the best watercress sprigs, chop the rest and mix with the turnips in a salad bowl. Whisk the remaining ingredients together until well blended, or put them in a screw-top jar and shake vigorously. Stir into the salad. Leave the salad to stand for about 15 minutes. Garnish with the reserved watercress before serving.

——————— *SERVES 4* ———————

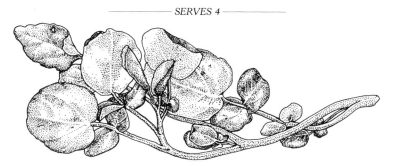

## SWEET GLAZED PEAS

*Illustrated facing page 48*

25 g (1 oz) BUTTER OR MARGARINE
5 SPRING ONIONS, CHOPPED
6 LETTUCE LEAVES, WASHED AND SHREDDED
350 g (12 oz) SHELLED PEAS
2 STICKS OF CELERY, WASHED, TRIMMED AND CHOPPED
SALT AND FRESHLY GROUND PEPPER
10 ml (2 TSP) LYLE'S GOLDEN SYRUP
CHOPPED PARSLEY TO GARNISH

M elt the fat in a saucepan, add the spring onion and cook for about 5 minutes until soft. Add the lettuce, peas, celery, seasoning and syrup. Cover and cook gently for 15–20 minutes, shaking the pan from time to time, until the peas are tender. Serve the peas hot, sprinkled with chopped parsley.

———————— *SERVES 4* ————————

## CELERY AND CRESS SALAD

*Illustrated between pages 40 and 41*

1 SMALL HEAD OF CELERY, TRIMMED AND WASHED
1 PUNNET OF CRESS
2 RED EATING APPLES, CORED AND THINLY SLICED
10 ml (2 LEVEL TSP) CARAWAY SEEDS
60 ml (4 TBSP) SOURED CREAM
15 ml (1 TBSP) LEMON JUICE
5 ml (1 TSP) LYLE'S GOLDEN SYRUP
1 GARLIC CLOVE, SKINNED AND CRUSHED
SALT AND FRESHLY GROUND PEPPER

S lice the celery and put it in a salad bowl with the cress, apples and caraway seeds. To make the dressing, whisk all the remaining ingredients together until well blended, or put them in a screw-top jar and shake vigorously. Stir into the salad before serving.

———————— *SERVES 4* ————————

# Glazed Beetroots

12 Small Beetroots, Cooked
25 g (1 oz) Butter or Margarine
15 ml (1 tbsp) Lyle's Golden Syrup
Salt and Freshly Ground Pepper
Grated Rind and Juice of ½ a Lemon
5 ml (1 tsp) Chopped Chives
10 ml (2 tsp) Chopped Parsley
15 ml (1 tbsp) Capers

Remove the skin, stalks and root end from the beetroots. Melt the fat in a saucepan and add the syrup, salt, pepper, lemon rind and juice. Boil for 5–10 minutes until thick. Add the beetroots, herbs and capers, heat through and serve immediately.

——— *SERVES 4* ———

# Pepper and Courgette Salad

*Illustrated between pages 40 and 41*

1 Yellow Pepper, Seeded and Finely Sliced
1 Red Pepper, Seeded and Finely Sliced
1 Green Pepper, Seeded and Finely Sliced
225 g (8 oz) Courgettes, Trimmed, Washed and Thinly Sliced
75 ml (5 tbsp) Sunflower Oil
45 ml (3 tbsp) Red Wine Vinegar
2.5 ml (½ tsp) Chilli Sauce
5 ml (1 tsp) Dijon Mustard
5 ml (1 tsp) Lyle's Golden Syrup
50 g (2 oz) Stuffed Green Olives, Sliced
Salt and Freshly Ground Pepper

Mix the peppers and courgettes in a serving bowl. Whisk the remaining ingredients together until well blended, or put them in a screw-top jar and shake vigorously. Combine with the peppers and courgettes. Leave the salad covered in the refrigerator to marinate overnight. Toss mixture thoroughly again before serving.

——— *SERVES 4–6* ———

# Tomato Coleslaw

*Illustrated opposite*

450 g (1 lb) White Cabbage, Trimmed and Shredded
1 Medium Red Pepper, Seeded and Sliced
4 Tomatoes, Skinned and Sliced
½ Cucumber, Sliced
300 ml (½ pint) Mayonnaise
60 ml (4 tbsp) Soured Cream
5 ml (1 tsp) Lyle's Golden Syrup
10 ml (2 tsp) Tomato Purée
Salt and Freshly Ground Pepper
Juice of 1 Lemon

Place the cabbage, pepper, tomatoes and cucumber in a salad bowl and mix well together. Beat the mayonnaise with the remaining ingredients and toss the salad ingredients in this dressing.

——————— SERVES 4 ———————

# Chicory Salad

*Illustrated opposite*

2 Medium Heads of Chicory, Trimmed and Finely Sliced
6 Black Olives, Stoned
30 ml (2 tbsp) Olive Oil
15 ml (1 tbsp) White Wine Vinegar
15 ml (1 tbsp) Lemon Juice
5 ml (1 tsp) Lyle's Golden Syrup
1 Small Onion, Skinned and Finely Grated
Salt and Freshly Ground Pepper

Put the chicory and olives into a bowl. To make the dressing, whisk all the remaining ingredients together until well blended, or put them in a screw-top jar and shake vigorously. Pour over the chicory and olives and toss well just before serving.

——————— SERVES 4 ———————

*Tomato coleslaw; Chicory salad.*
*Overleaf: Avocado salad with orange dressing; Celery and cress salad; Turnip and watercress salad; Pepper and courgette salad; Endive, orange and walnut salad.*

# BEAN SPROUT SALAD

*Illustrated opposite*

175 g (6 oz) BEAN SPROUTS, WASHED
1 MEDIUM RED PEPPER, SEEDED AND SLICED
3 SPRING ONIONS, CHOPPED
30 ml (2 TBSP) VEGETABLE OIL
15 ml (1 TBSP) WHITE WINE VINEGAR
10 ml (2 TSP) LYLE'S GOLDEN SYRUP
10 ml (2 TSP) SOY SAUCE

Mix the bean sprouts, red pepper and spring onions in a bowl. To make the dressing, whisk all the remaining ingredients together until well blended, or put them in a screw-top jar and shake vigorously. Pour the dressing over the bean sprouts and toss well. Leave to stand at room temperature for 30 minutes before serving to let the flavours blend.

———— *SERVES 2* ————

# CAULIFLOWER WITH SWEET AND SOUR SAUCE

*Illustrated facing page 48*

1 LARGE CAULIFLOWER
40 g (1½ oz) BUTTER OR MARGARINE
1 MEDIUM ONION, SKINNED AND FINELY CHOPPED
30 ml (2 TBSP) LYLE'S GOLDEN SYRUP
45 ml (3 TBSP) TOMATO PURÉE
30 ml (2 TBSP) WHITE WINE VINEGAR
10 ml (2 TSP) SOY SAUCE
60 ml (4 TBSP) WHITE WINE
SALT AND FRESHLY GROUND PEPPER

Divide the cauliflower into small florets and cook in a saucepan of boiling salted water for about 5 minutes until just tender. Drain well, put into a heated serving dish and keep warm. Melt the fat in a saucepan and fry the onion for 5 minutes, until soft.

Stir in all the remaining ingredients and cook for a further 3–4 minutes. Pour the sauce over the cauliflower.

———— *SERVES 4* ————

*Bean sprout salad; Mushroom, cucumber and coriander salad.*

# DESSERTS

## GOLDEN SYRUP ROLL

275 g (10 oz) SELF RAISING FLOUR
150 g (5 oz) SHREDDED SUET
75 g (3 oz) TATE & LYLE DEMERARA SUGAR
1 EGG
ABOUT 150 ml (¼ PINT) MILK
50 g (2 oz) FRESH WHITE BREADCRUMBS
225 g (8 oz) LYLE'S GOLDEN SYRUP
50 g (2 oz) WALNUTS, CHOPPED
LYLE'S GOLDEN SYRUP AND CLOTTED CREAM OR CUSTARD SAUCE TO
SERVE

Grease and line a baking sheet. In a mixing bowl, mix the flour, suet and 50 g (2 oz) sugar. Add the egg and enough milk to bind to a firm dough.

Roll out the dough on a floured work surface to an oblong about 38×30.5 cm (15×12 inches). Scatter over the breadcrumbs to within 2.5 cm (1 inch) of the edges. Spoon the golden syrup and half the nuts on top. Fold the edges of the dough up over the filling, dampen them and roll up from one short edge, sealing well.

Place seam-side down on the prepared baking sheet. Mix the remaining nuts and sugar together and scatter over the dough.

Bake in the oven at 180°C (350°F) mark 4 for about 1¼ hours until firm, cover lightly with foil when well browned. Transfer to a serving dish and spoon over golden syrup before serving with clotted cream or custard.

——————— *SERVES 6* ———————

# Refrigerated Cheesecake

50 g (2 oz) Butter or Margarine
75 ml (5 tbsp) Lyle's Golden Syrup
225 g (8 oz) Digestive Biscuits, Finely Crushed
225 g (8 oz) Cottage Cheese
225 g (8 oz) Full Fat Soft Cheese
Grated Rind and Juice of 2 Small Lemons
2 Eggs, Separated
15 ml (1 level tbsp) Gelatine
150 ml (¼ pint) Double Cream
Fresh Fruit such as Strawberries, Sliced, Kiwi Fruit, Peeled
and Sliced, Grapes, Halved and Pipped, to Decorate

Line the base of a 20.5-cm (8-inch) spring release cake tin with non-stick paper. Melt the fat and 30 ml (2 tbsp) syrup in a saucepan and stir in the biscuit crumbs until well mixed. Use this mixture to line the base of the prepared tin. Leave in the refrigerator for about 30 minutes until set.

Sieve the cottage cheese into a bowl and gradually beat in the soft cheese until smooth. Add the lemon rind and slowly work in 75 ml (5 tbsp) lemon juice. Whisk until smooth. Place the egg yolks and remaining syrup in a small bowl and whisk together until pale and thick, then gradually fold into the cheese mixture.

Place 45 ml (3 tbsp) water in a small bowl and sprinkle in the gelatine. Stand the bowl over a pan of hot water and heat gently until the gelatine dissolves. Stir into the cheese mixture. Whip the cream until stiff and fold into the cheese mixture. Finally, whisk the egg whites until stiff and fold into the mixture. Pour into the biscuit case, smooth surface and leave in refrigerator for 2–3 hours to set.

About 20 minutes before serving, carefully remove the cheesecake from the tin. Decorate with fresh fruit.

*——— SERVES 6–8 ———*

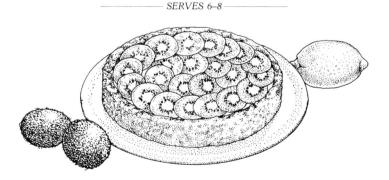

# Delaware Pudding

30 ml (2 tbsp) Lyle's Golden Syrup
100 g (4 oz) Butter or Margarine
100 g (4 oz) Tate & Lyle Caster Sugar
2 Eggs, Beaten
175 g (6 oz) Self Raising Flour
30 ml (2 tbsp) Milk
225 g (8 oz) Cooking Apples, Peeled, Cored and Sliced
50 g (2 oz) Tate & Lyle Demerara Sugar
50 g (2 oz) Currants
5 ml (1 level tsp) Cinnamon
Single Cream or Custard to Serve

Grease a 1.1-litre (2-pint) round pie dish and put the syrup in the base. Cream the fat and sugar until pale and fluffy. Add the egg a little at a time, beating well after each addition. Fold in half the flour and all the milk, using a metal spoon, then fold in the remaining flour. Mix the remaining ingredients together in a separate bowl.

Put a thin layer of the sponge mixture on to the syrup, then half of the spicy apple, then another thin layer of sponge, and then the remainder of the apples. Finally, put a thicker layer of sponge on the top and smooth over. Cover with greased greaseproof paper or foil and secure with string. Steam for about 1¾ hours until well risen and firm to the touch. Unmould the pudding and serve with single cream or custard.

——————— *SERVES 4–6* ———————

# Dried Fruit Fool

450 g (1 lb) Dried Fruit such as Apricots, Peaches, Pears, Prunes,
Apples, Soaked Overnight
150 ml (¼ pint) Double Cream
15 ml (1 tbsp) Lyle's Golden Syrup
Chopped Walnuts to Decorate

Drain the fruit and place in a blender or food processor with the cream and syrup. Blend until smooth (it may be necessary to blend half the mixture at a time). Spoon into six individual dishes and chill. Serve decorated with walnuts.

——————— *SERVES 6* ———————

# Gooseberry Mallow Ice Cream

*Illustrated between pages 56 and 57*

12 White Marshmallows
170-g (6-oz) Can Evaporated Milk
225 g (8 oz) Fresh or Frozen Gooseberries, Topped and Tailed
45 ml (3 tbsp) Lyle's Golden Syrup
150 ml (¼ pint) Double Cream, Lightly Whipped
Chocolate Fudge Sauce (See Page 91)

P lace the marshmallows and evaporated milk in a small bowl and then stand the bowl in a pan of warm water to melt the marshmallows. Stir until smooth, then leave until cool. Place the gooseberries in a saucepan with 30 ml (2 tbsp) water. Cover and cook gently for about 5 minutes, or until the skins burst and the fruit softens. Stir the syrup into the warm fruit then purée in a blender or food processor until just smooth.

Leave until cool, then stir into the marshmallow mixture with the cream. Spoon into a deep freezer-proof container and freeze until required. There is no need to beat the mixture during freezing.

To serve, leave the ice cream to soften in the refrigerator for 45–60 minutes. Serve the ice cream in individual dishes with Chocolate fudge sauce poured over the top.

*SERVES 6–8*

# Mixed Fruit Roly Poly

225 g (8 oz) Self Raising Flour
2.5 ml (½ level tsp) Salt
100 g (4 oz) Shredded Suet
15 g (½ oz) Butter or Margarine
45 ml (3 tbsp) Lyle's Golden Syrup
15 ml (1 level tbsp) Tate & Lyle Dark Brown Soft Sugar
75 g (3 oz) Currants
50 g (2 oz) Sultanas
50 g (2 oz) Seedless Raisins
1.25 ml (¼ level tsp) Ground Allspice
Grated Rind of 1 Lemon
Milk for Brushing
Custard to Serve

Mix together the flour, salt and suet in a bowl. Add enough cold water to give a light, elastic dough and knead very lightly until smooth. Roll out the pastry on a floured work surface to about 20.5×25.5 cm (8×10 inches).

Melt the fat, golden syrup and sugar in a saucepan and stir in the fruit, spice and lemon rind. Spread the fruit mixture on the pastry, leaving about 1 cm (½ inch) border along each edge. Brush the edges with milk and roll the pastry up evenly, starting from one short side. Pinch the ends to seal.

Place on a baking sheet and bake in the oven at 200°C (400°F) mark 6 for about 1 hour, until firm and golden. Serve hot with pouring custard.

———— *SERVES 4* ————

# Pancakes with Orange and Syrup

100 g (4 oz) Plain Flour
1.25 ml (¼ level tsp) Salt
1 Egg, Beaten
150 ml (¼ pint) Milk
Vegetable Oil
45 ml (3 tbsp) Lyle's Golden Syrup
15 ml (1 tbsp) Lemon Juice
2 Oranges, Peeled and Segmented
2 Bananas, Peeled and Sliced

Sift the flour and salt together into a bowl. Make a well in the centre and gradually pour in the egg and milk, beating after each addition. Beat until the batter is smooth, then add 150 ml (¼ pint) water.

Heat 2.5 ml (½ tsp) vegetable oil in a small frying pan. When very hot, pour off the excess oil and pour in enough batter to thinly coat the base of the pan. Cook gently until the underside of the pancake is golden brown. Turn it over and cook the second side until golden brown. Turn out on to greaseproof paper and keep warm. Repeat with the rest of the batter until eight pancakes are made, oiling the pan again when necessary.

Heat the syrup and lemon juice in a saucepan and stir in the orange segments and banana slices. Coat well in the syrup, then divide equally on to the centre of each hot pancake. Carefully flip two sides of each pancake over the filling and serve immediately.

———— MAKES 8 ————

# Baked Apples

4 Medium Cooking Apples
60 ml (4 tbsp) Lyle's Golden Syrup
Butter

Wipe the apples and make a shallow cut through the skin round the middle of each. Core the apples and stand them in an ovenproof dish. Pour 60 ml (4 tbsp) water round them, fill each apple with golden syrup and top with a small knob of butter. Bake in the oven at 200°C (400°F) mark 6 for 45–60 minutes until the apples are soft.

———— SERVES 4 ————

## RASPBERRY ICE CREAM

*Illustrated between pages 56 and 57*

450 g (1 lb) FRESH OR FROZEN RASPBERRIES
30 ml (2 TBSP) LYLE'S GOLDEN SYRUP
410-g (14.5-oz) CAN EVAPORATED MILK, CHILLED
150 ml (¼ PINT) WHIPPING CREAM
45 ml (3 TBSP) LEMON JUICE

Pick over the fresh raspberries, wash and drain well. Place berries in a small saucepan with the syrup, cover the pan and cook gently until the fruit is soft and pulpy. Purée in a blender, then rub through a nylon sieve and leave to cool.

Whip the evaporated milk until it thickens slightly, then whip the cream to the same consistency, and fold gently together. Stir in the cold fruit purée and the lemon juice. Pour into a shallow container (not metal), so that the ice cream mixture comes about 3.5 cm (1½ inches) up the sides.

Freeze for about 3 hours, or until set to a mushy consistency, then beat well to break down the ice crystals. Return to the freezer for at least 6 hours. Allow to soften in the refrigerator for 2 hours before serving.

*SERVES 6*

## CHINESE STEAMED CAKE

2 EGGS
25 g (1 oz) TATE & LYLE LIGHT BROWN SOFT SUGAR
25 g (1 oz) LYLE'S GOLDEN SYRUP
75 ml (5 TBSP) MILK
125 g (4 oz) SELF RAISING FLOUR
15 ml (1 TBSP) VEGETABLE OIL
GRATED RIND OF 1 ORANGE
LYLE'S GOLDEN SYRUP TO SERVE

Grease an 18-cm (7-inch) round cake tin. Beat the eggs in a mixing bowl, and stir in the sugar, syrup and milk. Fold in the flour and mix together well. Add the oil and orange rind. Pour mixture into tin, cover with greased grease-proof paper or foil and secure with string. Steam in a steamer for 20–30 minutes.

Remove the cake from the tin while still hot. Cut into squares and drizzle over the syrup. Serve hot or cold.

*SERVES 4*

*Cauliflower with sweet and sour sauce; Sweet glazed peas.*

# Butterscotch Cream

*Illustrated opposite*

50 g (2 oz) Cornflour
568 ml (1 pint) Milk
15 ml (1 tbsp) Lyle's Golden Syrup
25 g (1 oz) Tate & Lyle Dark Brown Soft Sugar
25 g (1 oz) Butter
50 g (2 oz) Glacé Cherries, Roughly Chopped
25 g (1 oz) Walnuts, Chopped

In a bowl, blend the cornflour with a little of the milk to make a smooth paste. In a saucepan, heat the remaining milk with the syrup, sugar and butter until well blended. Stir into the cornflour paste and return to the pan. Bring to the boil, stirring continuously until the mixture thickens.

Pour into individual dishes and sprinkle with cherries and nuts. Serve hot.

—————— SERVES 4 ——————

# Spiced Blackberry Layer

450 g (1 lb) Blackberries
60 ml (4 tbsp) Lyle's Golden Syrup
175 g (6 oz) Butter or Margarine
175 g (6 oz) Tate & Lyle Caster Sugar
3 Eggs, Beaten
175 g (6 oz) Self Raising Flour
2.5 ml (½ level tsp) Ground Mixed Spice
15–30 ml (1–2 tbsp) Milk
Whipped Cream for Serving

Place the blackberries in a 20.5×28 cm (8×11 inch) greased ovenproof dish and spoon over the golden syrup. Cream together the fat and sugar until light and fluffy. Beat in the eggs a little at a time. Fold in the flour and mixed spice. Add just enough milk to mix to a soft dropping consistency. Spread over the top of the blackberries.

Cook in the oven at 180°C (350°F) mark 4 for 45 minutes, until risen and golden brown. Serve hot with whipped cream.

—————— SERVES 6 ——————

*Butterscotch cream; Plum mousse.*

# Golden Rice with Dates

568 ml (1 pint) Milk
65 g (2½ oz) Pudding (Short Grain) Rice
25 g (1 oz) Tate & Lyle Caster Sugar
1 Egg, Beaten
25 g (1 oz) Shredded Suet
75 g (3 oz) Dried Dates, Chopped
30 ml (2 tbsp) Lyle's Golden Syrup
Lyle's Golden Syrup to Serve

Grease and base line six 5.5-cm (2¼-inch) deep dariole moulds. Place the milk, rice and sugar together in a saucepan. Bring to the boil, simmer gently, stirring occasionally for about 25 minutes until the rice is cooked and the mixture soft and creamy. Cool slightly, then beat in the egg and suet.

Press equal amounts of the dates into the base of each mould. Spoon a little golden syrup over the dates in each. Divide the rice mixture between the prepared moulds. Stand in a deep cake tin filled with enough water to come halfway up their sides. Cover with greased greaseproof paper and foil. Tie securely.

Bake in the oven at 170°C (325°F) mark 3 for about 50 minutes, or until just firm to the touch. Uncover, turn out on to a warmed serving dish. Serve with warm golden syrup.

*SERVES 6*

# Orange Sherbet

*Illustrated between pages 56 and 57*

178-ml (6¼-oz) Carton Frozen Orange Juice
175 g (6 oz) Tate & Lyle Caster Sugar
45 ml (3 tbsp) Lyle's Golden Syrup
45 ml (3 tbsp) Lemon Juice
568 ml (1 pint) Milk
300 ml (½ pint) Single Cream

Turn out the frozen, undiluted orange juice into a deep bowl. When beginning to soften add the sugar, golden syrup and lemon juice, and whisk until smooth. Stir in the milk and cream, and pour into a deep container, cover and freeze. There is no need to beat the mixture during freezing. Transfer to the refrigerator 45–60 minutes before serving.

*SERVES 8*

# WALNUT TART

175 g (6 oz) PLAIN FLOUR
PINCH OF SALT
40 g (1½ oz) BUTTER OR BLOCK MARGARINE
40 g (1½ oz) LARD
100 g (4 oz) WALNUTS, CHOPPED
3 EGGS, BEATEN
150 ml (¼ PINT) LYLE'S GOLDEN SYRUP
50 g (2 oz) MARGARINE, MELTED
GRATED RIND AND JUICE OF 1 ORANGE
75 g (3 oz) TATE & LYLE DARK BROWN SOFT SUGAR
CREAM TO SERVE

Place the flour and salt in a bowl and rub in the fats until the mixture resembles fine breadcrumbs. Mix to a smooth dough with about 30 ml (2 tbsp) water. Roll out the pastry on a floured work surface and use to line a 19-cm (7½-inch) loose-bottomed flan tin. Beat together all the remaining ingredients, except the cream, and pour into the flan.

Bake in the oven at 180°C (350°F) mark 4 for 50–60 minutes until golden brown and firm to the touch. Serve hot or cold with cream.

————— *SERVES 6* —————

# Plum Mousse

*Illustrated facing page 49*

450 g (1 lb) Plums, Halved and Stoned
30 ml (2 tbsp) Lyle's Golden Syrup
Grated Rind and Juice of 1 Lemon
75 g (3 oz) Tate & Lyle Demerara Sugar
350 g (12 oz) Curd Cheese
142-ml (5-fl oz) Carton Soured Cream
15 ml (1 level tbsp) Gelatine
2 Egg Whites
Natural Yogurt to Serve

Put the plums, syrup, lemon rind and juice and the sugar in a saucepan and simmer for about 20 minutes until the plums are soft and pulpy. Rub through a sieve or liquidise in a blender to form a purée. Beat the curd cheese and soured cream together.

Put 60 ml (4 tbsp) water in a small bowl and sprinkle in the gelatine. Stand the bowl over a pan of hot water and heat gently until the gelatine has dissolved. Stir into the plum mixture and leave to cool. Gradually beat the plum mixture into the cheese mixture and leave until beginning to set, then stiffly whisk the egg whites and fold into the mixture. Pour into a dampened 1.1-litre (2-pint) jelly mould and leave to set in the refrigerator for about 2 hours. Turn out and serve with natural yogurt.

———— *SERVES 4–6* ————

# Strawberry Refrigerator Cake

225 g (8 oz) Strawberries, Hulled and Sliced
150 ml (¼ pint) Fresh Orange Juice
45 ml (3 tbsp) Orange-flavoured Liqueur
30 ml (2 level tbsp) Tate & Lyle Icing Sugar
30 ml (2 tbsp) Lyle's Golden Syrup
2 Egg Yolks, Beaten
75 g (3 oz) Butter or Margarine
30 Boudoir Biscuits
150 ml (¼ pint) Double Cream
60 ml (4 tbsp) Single Cream
Whole Strawberries to Decorate

Place the strawberries in a shallow bowl. Mix the orange juice, liqueur and sugar, pour over the strawberries and leave for 30 minutes. Place the golden syrup in a small saucepan over a gentle heat, bring to the boil, then allow to cool for 1 minute. Pour in a thin stream on to the egg yolks, whisking all the time; continue to whisk until pale and creamy. Cream the fat until soft, then beat in the egg syrup, a little at a time. Drain the strawberries, reserving the marinade.

Dip ten boudoir biscuits in the orange marinade and arrange them side by side on a sheet of non-stick paper. Cover with a layer of half the butter filling. Top with half the marinated strawberries. Add another layer of ten biscuits, dipped in the marinade, and top with the remaining butter mixture and strawberries. Finally, top with a layer of biscuits, dipped in the last of the marinade. Wrap the cake in paper and chill in the refrigerator.

About 30 minutes before serving, put both creams in a bowl and whip until the cream mixture is thick enough to hold its shape. Cover the cake completely with the cream and decorate with whole strawberries.

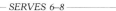

*SERVES 6–8*

# ICED PINEAPPLE CRUSH

125 g (4 oz) BUTTER OR MARGARINE
125 g (4 oz) PLAIN CHOCOLATE FLAVOUR CAKE COVERING
30 ml (2 TBSP) LYLE'S GOLDEN SYRUP
225 g (8 oz) DIGESTIVE BISCUITS, CRUSHED
450 ml (¾ PINT) DOUBLE CREAM
THREE 250-g (8½-oz) CANS CRUSHED PINEAPPLE
45 ml (3 TBSP) LEMON JUICE
40 g (1½ oz) TATE & LYLE ICING SUGAR, SIFTED
FRESH OR CANNED PINEAPPLE TO DECORATE

Base line a 28 × 18 × 2.5 cm (11 × 7 × 1 inch) deep tin with non-stick paper. Melt the fat, cake covering and syrup together in a small saucepan. Stir in the crushed biscuits, then press the crumb mixture into the tin. Place in the refrigerator and leave until set.

Lightly whip the cream and fold in the drained crushed pineapple, lemon juice and icing sugar. Spread the pineapple mixture over the biscuit base and freeze for at least 3 hours until firm.

Allow to soften at cool room temperature for 10–15 minutes before serving. Decorate with pineapple and serve cut into wedges or squares.

*SERVES 10*

# MIDDLE EASTERN WHEAT IN SYRUP

225 g (8 oz) WHOLEWHEAT GRAIN
175 g (6 oz) LYLE'S GOLDEN SYRUP
30 ml (2 TBSP) LEMON JUICE
5–10 ml (1–2 TSP) ROSE WATER
SLIVERED ALMONDS AND PISTACHIO NUTS TO DECORATE

Place the wheat in a saucepan and cover with water. Bring to the boil, and boil for about 1 hour until tender and the grains begin to open. Drain well and put into a heatproof serving dish.

Put the golden syrup, 150 ml (¼ pint) water and lemon juice in a pan and heat gently. Simmer for 10 minutes to form a syrup thick enough to coat the back of a wooden spoon. Add the rose water and pour over the wheat. Leave to cool then decorate with nuts.

*SERVES 4*

# Profiteroles

*Illustrated on the jacket and facing page 64*

50 g (2 oz) Block Margarine
65 g (2½ oz) Plain Flour
2 Eggs, Lightly Beaten
150 ml (¼ pint) Double Cream
Tate & Lyle Icing Sugar for Dusting

———— *For the chocolate sauce* ————
100 g (4 oz) Plain Chocolate
15 g (½ oz) Butter
30 ml (2 tbsp) Lyle's Golden Syrup
2–3 Drops Vanilla Flavouring

Place the margarine in a saucepan with 150 ml (¼ pint) water. Heat until the margarine is melted then bring to the boil. Remove from the heat and quickly tip in the flour all at once. Beat with a wooden spoon until the paste is smooth and forms a ball in the centre of the pan. Allow to cool for a minute or two. Beat in the egg a little at a time, beating vigorously.

Lightly grease two baking sheets. Using a piping bag fitted with a 1-cm (½-inch) plain nozzle, pipe about twenty small bun shapes on the prepared baking sheets.

Bake in the oven at 200°C (400°F) mark 6 for about 25 minutes until well risen and golden brown. Make a hole in the side of each bun with a skewer or knife and cool on a wire rack.

For the chocolate sauce, melt the chocolate with the butter in a small saucepan over a very low heat. Add 30 ml (2 tbsp) water, the syrup and vanilla flavouring, stir well until smooth and well blended.

Whip the double cream and use to fill the choux buns. Dust with icing sugar and serve with the chocolate sauce spooned over or served separately.

———— *SERVES 4* ————

## CRANBERRY PUDDING

*Illustrated opposite*

225 g (8 oz) Fresh Cranberrries, Chopped
175 g (6 oz) Self Raising Flour
2.5 ml (½ level tsp) Bicarbonate of Soda
Pinch of Salt
50 g (2 oz) Shredded Suet
50 g (2 oz) Tate & Lyle Dark Brown Soft Sugar
5 ml (1 tsp) Lyle's Black Treacle
50 g (2 oz) Lyle's Golden Syrup
1 Egg, Size 2, Beaten
Toffee Sauce to Serve (See Page 92)

Grease a 900-ml (1½-pint) pudding basin. In a bowl combine the cranberries with the flour, bicarbonate of soda and salt. Stir in the suet and sugar. Make a hollow in the centre, and add the black treacle, syrup and egg. Gradually work in the dry ingredients and mix well. Put the mixture into the basin, cover with greased greaseproof paper or foil and secure with string. Steam over a pan of boiling water for about 2½–3 hours until well risen and firm to the touch. Serve with Toffee sauce or cream.

———— *SERVES 6* ————

## GOLDEN SPONGE PUDDING

*Illustrated facing page 57*

45 ml (3 tbsp) Lyle's Golden Syrup
100 g (4 oz) Butter or Margarine
100 g (4 oz) Tate & Lyle Caster Sugar
2 Eggs, Beaten
Grated Rind of 1 Lemon
175 g (6 oz) Self Raising Flour, Sifted
15–30 ml (1–2 tbsp) Milk

Grease a 900-ml (1½-pint) pudding basin. Put the syrup in the bottom of the basin. In a bowl, cream together the fat and sugar until pale and fluffy. Add the beaten eggs, a little at a time and beat well after each addition. Add the lemon rind. Using a metal spoon, fold in half the sifted flour, then fold in the rest, with enough milk to give a dropping consistency. Put the mixture into the basin, cover with greased greaseproof paper or foil and secure with string. Steam over a pan of boiling water for 1½ hours until well risen and firm to the touch.

———— *SERVES 4–6* ————

*Cranberry pudding and Toffee sauce.*
*Overleaf: Raspberry ice cream; Orange sherbet; Gooseberry mallow ice cream and Chocolate fudge sauce.*

# Tipsy Syrup Tart

*Illustrated opposite*

100 g (4 oz) Fresh White Breadcrumbs
225 g (8 oz) Lyle's Golden Syrup
30 ml (2 tbsp) Dark Rum
100 g (4 oz) Butter or Block Margarine
225 g (8 oz) Plain Flour
1 Egg, Separated
Tate & Lyle Caster Sugar for Dusting
Cream to Serve

Lightly grease a 22-cm (8½-inch) loose-bottomed fluted French flan tin. Put the breadcrumbs in a large bowl, add the syrup and rum and stir until mixed. In another bowl, rub the fat into the flour until it resembles fine breadcrumbs. Mix the egg yolk with 30 ml (2 tbsp) water and use it to bind the pastry mixture to a firm dough. Roll out three-quarters of the pastry on a floured work surface and use to line the prepared tin. Spoon in the syrup mixture. Roll out the remaining pastry into a narrow strip, cut into thin strips and arrange in a lattice pattern over the top.

Bake in the oven at 180°C (350°F) mark 4 for about 20 minutes or until just set but not browned. Brush the pastry lattice with lightly beaten egg white and sprinkle with caster sugar. Return to the oven for a further 15–20 minutes or until well browned. Ease out of the flan tin and serve warm with cream.

*SERVES 6*

*Golden sponge pudding; Tipsy syrup tart.*

# CAKES AND
# TEABREADS

## FRUIT CRUSTED CIDER CAKE

*Illustrated between pages 72 and 73*

45 ml (3 TBSP) LYLE'S GOLDEN SYRUP
150 g (5 oz) BUTTER OR BLOCK MARGARINE
350 g (12 oz) COOKING APPLES, PEELED, CORED AND FINELY CHOPPED
45 ml (3 TBSP) MINCEMEAT
50 g (2 oz) CORNFLAKES, CRUSHED
125 g (4 oz) TATE & LYLE CASTER SUGAR
2 EGGS, BEATEN
125 g (4 oz) SELF RAISING FLOUR, SIFTED
45 ml (3 TBSP) DRY CIDER

Grease and line a 28 × 18 cm (11 × 7 inch) rectangular baking tin. Melt the syrup and 25 g (1 oz) fat gently together and stir in the apple, mincemeat and cornflakes.

Cream together the remaining fat and sugar until pale and fluffy. Gradually beat in the eggs. Fold in the flour and lastly the cider.

Spoon the creamed mixture into the prepared tin and smooth over the surface with a palette knife. Spread the apple topping evenly over the cake surface. Bake in the oven at 170°C (325°F) mark 3 for about 45–50 minutes or until firm to the touch.

Leave to cool in the tin, then cut into bars for serving.

*SERVES 8*

# Syrup Teabread

*Illustrated between pages 72 and 73*

175 g (6 oz) Self Raising Flour
5 ml (1 level tsp) Ground Cinnamon
Pinch of Salt
45 ml (3 tbsp) Vegetable Oil
60 ml (4 tbsp) Lyle's Golden Syrup
50 g (2 oz) Tate & Lyle Demerara Sugar
1 Egg
30 ml (2 tbsp) Milk
75 g (3 oz) Sultanas

——— *For the topping* ———
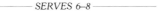
15 ml (1 tbsp) Lyle's Golden Syrup, Warmed
15 g (½ oz) Glacé Cherries, Chopped
15 g (½ oz) Walnuts

Grease and base line a 750-ml (1¼-pint) loaf tin measuring 15 × 8.5 cm (6 × 3½ inches) across the top.

Sift together the flour, cinnamon and salt into a large bowl. Add the remaining ingredients, except the topping ingredients, mix well and beat for 2–3 minutes until well blended. Pour the mixture into the prepared tin and bake in the oven at 180°C (350°F) mark 4 for 1 hour, cover with foil if the cake becomes too dark. Cool in the tin for a few minutes, then turn out and leave to finish cooling on a wire rack.

For the topping, brush the top of the cake with syrup, then sprinkle over the cherries and nuts.

Serve sliced and spread with butter.

——— *SERVES 6–8* ———

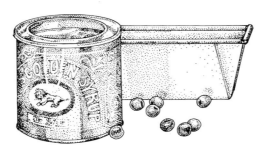

# Syrup Almond Loaf

275 g (10 oz) Self Raising Flour
2.5 ml (½ level tsp) Salt
50 g (2 oz) Butter
50 g (2 oz) White Vegetable Fat, Not Lard
50 g (2 oz) Tate & Lyle Caster Sugar
1 Egg, Beaten
100 ml (4 fl oz) Milk
60 ml (4 tbsp) Lyle's Golden Syrup
50 g (2 oz) Ground Almonds
50 g (2 oz) Sultanas
Finely Grated Rind of 1 Orange

———— *For the icing* ————
100 g (4 oz) Tate & Lyle Icing Sugar, Sifted
20 ml (4 tsp) Milk
Few Drops of Vanilla Flavouring

Grease and base line a 1.1-litre (2-pint) loaf tin. Sift the flour with the salt, and rub in the fats until the mixture resembles breadcrumbs. Stir in the caster sugar, egg and milk.

With floured hands roll into thirty 2.5-cm (1-inch) balls. Place half in the base of the loaf tin (five rows of three balls each). Mix 30 ml (2 tbsp) syrup with the ground almonds, sultanas and orange rind and spoon over the balls in the tin. Top with the remaining balls and drizzle with the rest of the syrup.

Bake in the oven at 190°C (375°F) mark 5 for about 50 minutes until risen and firm to the touch, covering loosely with foil after 25 minutes.

Meanwhile, combine the ingredients to make the icing. Turn the cake out of the tin and spoon over the icing while still warm.

Keep for 2 days before eating, thickly sliced and spread with butter.

———— *SERVES 8* ————

# Apple Gingerbread Ring

*Illustrated between pages 72 and 73*

225 g (8 oz) Plain Flour
2.5 ml (½ level tsp) Salt
7.5 ml (1½ level tsp) Ground Ginger
7.5 ml (1½ level tsp) Baking Powder
2.5 ml (½ level tsp) Bicarbonate of Soda
100 g (4 oz) Tate & Lyle Light Brown Soft Sugar
75 g (3 oz) Butter or Margarine
25 g (1 oz) Lyle's Black Treacle
100 g (4 oz) Lyle's Golden Syrup
150 ml (¼ pint) Milk
1 Egg, Beaten
3 Eating Apples, Cored, Peeled and Sliced
16 Whole Stoned Dates
2 Large Pieces of Preserved Stem Ginger, Cut into Thin Strips

———— *For the glaze* ————
50 g (2 oz) Lyle's Golden Syrup
2.5 ml (½ level tsp) Ground Ginger
10 ml (2 level tsp) Arrowroot
30 ml (2 tbsp) Preserved Stem Ginger Syrup

Grease and line a 1.4-litre (2½-pint) ring mould or a 20.5-cm (8-inch) round deep cake tin. Place a foil-wrapped 5-cm (2-inch) diameter empty can in the centre of the cake tin. Sift the flour, salt, ground ginger, baking powder and bicarbonate of soda into a large mixing bowl. Put the sugar, fat, treacle and syrup in a saucepan and heat gently, until the fat melts. Pour the milk into a small pan and warm slightly, then beat in the egg. Add the treacle and milk mixtures to the dry ingredients. Mix thoroughly and pour into the prepared tin.

Bake in the oven at 180°C (350°F) mark 4 for 35 minutes or until well risen. Remove the can, if used, and turn out the cake. Cool on a wire rack.

For the glaze, put the syrup and 150 ml (¼ pint) water in a saucepan, bring to the boil and simmer for 5 minutes. Blend together the ground ginger and arrowroot with the ginger syrup. Pour on the hot syrup, stir well and return to the pan. Continue boiling and stirring for 2 minutes. Add the apples to the pan and poach in the glaze for 10–15 minutes or until just tender.

Arrange the apples, dates and ginger in the centre of the cake and brush the glaze over the cake.

———— *SERVES 8* ————

## Banana Teabread

200 g (7 oz) Self Raising Flour
1.25 ml (¼ level tsp) Bicarbonate of Soda
2.5 ml (½ level tsp) Salt
75 g (3 oz) Butter or Block Margarine
100 g (4 oz) Tate & Lyle Caster Sugar
2 Eggs, Beaten
225 g (8 oz) Bananas, Peeled and Mashed
30 ml (2 tbsp) Lyle's Golden Syrup
225 g (8 oz) Mixed Dried Fruit
100 g (4 oz) Nuts, Coarsely Chopped

Grease and line a 1.4-litre (2½-pint) loaf tin measuring 19 × 11 cm (7½ × 4½ inches) across the top. Sift together the flour, bicarbonate of soda and salt into a bowl. Rub the fat into the flour until the mixture resembles fine breadcrumbs. Stir in the sugar. Beat the eggs, banana and golden syrup together and then stir into the mixture. Stir in the dried fruit and nuts.

Turn into the prepared tin and bake in the oven at 180°C (350°F) mark 4 for about 1¼ hours until well risen and just firm. Turn out and cool on a wire rack.

Wrap in foil and keep for a day before serving sliced and buttered.

———————— *SERVES 8* ————————

# APPLE AND WALNUT TEABREAD

225 g (8 oz) SELF RAISING FLOUR
PINCH OF SALT
5 ml (1 LEVEL TSP) MIXED SPICE
100 g (4 oz) SOFT TUB MARGARINE
100 g (4 oz) TATE & LYLE CASTER SUGAR
2 EGGS, SIZE 2
15 ml (1 TBSP) LYLE'S GOLDEN SYRUP
100 g (4 oz) SULTANAS
50 g (2 oz) WALNUTS, CHOPPED
1 MEDIUM COOKING APPLE, PEELED, CORED AND CHOPPED

Grease and line a 1.4-litre (2½-pint) loaf tin measuring 19 × 11 cm (7½ × 4½ inches) across the top. Sift together the flour, salt and mixed spice into a large bowl. Add the remaining ingredients and beat together until well blended.

Turn the mixture into the prepared tin and bake in the oven at 180°C (350°F) mark 4 for 1 hour. Reduce the oven temperature to 170°C (325°F) mark 3 and bake for a further 20 minutes. Turn out and leave to cool on a wire rack.

———————— *SERVES 8* ————————

# PEANUT AND ORANGE TEABREAD

*Illustrated facing page 72*

226-g (8-oz) JAR CHUNKY PEANUT BUTTER
50 g (2 oz) BUTTER OR MARGARINE, SOFTENED
275 g (10 oz) SELF RAISING FLOUR
1.25 ml (¼ LEVEL TSP) SALT
100 g (4 oz) LYLE'S GOLDEN SYRUP
2 EGGS
GRATED RIND AND JUICE OF 2 ORANGES
MILK
50 g (2 oz) SALTED PEANUTS

Grease and line a loaf tin measuring 24 × 14 cm (9½ × 5½ inches). In a large, deep bowl place the peanut butter, fat, flour, salt, syrup, eggs and grated orange rind. Make the orange juice up to 225 ml (8 fl oz) with milk. Add to bowl and beat all together with a wooden spoon for about 3 minutes.

Turn into the tin. Sprinkle with peanuts and bake in the oven at 180°C (350°F) mark 4 for about 1¼ hours. Turn out and cool on a wire rack.

———————— *SERVES 8* ————————

# Syrup Nut Stick

15 g (½ oz) Fresh Yeast or 7.5 ml (1½ level tsp) Dried Yeast and 5
ml (1 level tsp) Tate & Lyle Caster Sugar
About 300 ml (½ pint) Tepid Milk
450 g (1 lb) Strong Plain Flour
5 ml (1 level tsp) Salt
50 g (2 oz) Butter
75 ml (5 tbsp) Lyle's Golden Syrup
90 ml (6 tbsp) Crunchy Peanut Butter
Beaten Egg
Sesame Seeds
Lyle's Golden Syrup for Glazing

Blend the fresh yeast with the milk. If using dried yeast, dissolve the sugar in
the milk, sprinkle the yeast over and leave for about 10 minutes until frothy.
Mix the flour and salt and rub in the butter. Make a well in the centre and add the
yeast liquid. Stir in 15 ml (1 tbsp) golden syrup. Mix to an elastic dough, adding
more milk if necessary.

Turn on to a floured work surface, and knead for at least 10 minutes until
smooth and elastic. Shape into a ball and place in a clean, oiled mixing bowl.
Stretch oiled cling film over the top of the bowl. Leave in a warm place until
doubled in size. Knead again for 4–5 minutes.

Roll out dough on a floured work surface to a rectangle 33 × 23 cm (13 ×
9 inches). Spread with the peanut butter, leaving 2.5 cm (1 inch) dough round the
edges. Spread the remaining golden syrup on top.

Roll up like a Swiss roll from the long edge. Place on a greased baking sheet
and scissor snip to make deep diagonal slashes at 5-cm (2-inch) intervals along the
loaf. Open out the leaves of dough slightly.

Cover with oiled cling film and leave in a warm place until doubled in size.
Brush with beaten egg and scatter over the sesame seeds.

Bake in the oven at 220°C (425°F) mark 7 for 25–30 minutes until browned
and risen. Brush with syrup while still warm. Cool on a wire rack.

*SERVES 6–8*

*Profiteroles.*

# BUTTERSCOTCH CAKE

*Illustrated opposite*

100 g (4 oz) Butter or Margarine
175 g (6 oz) Tate & Lyle Light Brown Soft Sugar
2 Eggs, Separated
15 ml (1 tbsp) Lyle's Golden Syrup
120 ml (8 tbsp) Milk
2.5 ml (½ tsp) Vanilla Flavouring
225 g (8 oz) Self Raising Flour
Pinch of Salt

———— *For the caramel icing* ————
225 g (8 oz) Tate & Lyle Light Brown Soft Sugar
30 ml (2 tbsp) Milk
25 g (1 oz) Butter

———— *For the decoration* ————
Whole Almonds and Walnuts
Lyle's Golden Syrup, Warmed

Grease and base line an 18-cm (7-inch) square cake tin. Cream together the fat and sugar, then beat the egg yolks into the creamed mixture. Stir in the syrup, milk and flavouring. Sift the flour and salt on top of mixture then fold in. Beat the egg whites until stiff, then fold gently into the mixture.

Put the mixture into the prepared cake tin and bake in the oven at 180°C (350°F) mark 4 for about 1 hour. Remove from tin and cool on a wire rack.

To make the caramel icing, put all the ingredients into a saucepan. Bring slowly to the boil, stirring. Boil gently for 5 minutes to 116°C (240°F) (soft ball stage), then remove from the heat. Beat until creamy. Spread on top of the cake with a wet knife.

To decorate, place the whole nuts around the top edge of the cake, and brush them with a little syrup to glaze.

———————— *SERVES 6–8* ————————

*Frosted carrot cake; Butterscotch cake.*

# Apricot Tea Loaf

225 g (8 oz) Dried Apricots
100 g (4 oz) Tate & Lyle Caster Sugar
75 g (3 oz) Lard
2.5 ml (½ level tsp) Ground Cinnamon
2.5 ml (½ level tsp) Ground Cloves
1.25 ml (¼ level tsp) Grated Nutmeg
2.5 ml (½ level tsp) Salt
225 g (8 oz) Plain Flour
5 ml (1 level tsp) Bicarbonate of Soda
2 Eggs, Beaten
45 ml (3 tbsp) Lyle's Golden Syrup

Grease and line a loaf tin measuring 23 × 12.5 × 6.5 cm (9 × 5 × 2½ inches). Cut the apricots into small pieces and place in a saucepan with 300 ml (½ pint) water, less 30 ml (2 tbsp). Add the sugar, lard, spices and salt. Simmer for 5 minutes, then leave until cold.

Sift together the flour and bicarbonate of soda. Make a well in the centre, stir in the apricot mixture, the eggs and the golden syrup, mix well, then pour into the prepared tin.

Bake in the oven at 180°C (350°F) mark 4 for about 1–1¼ hours until well risen and firm to the touch. Turn out and cool on a wire rack.

Slice thinly and spread with butter to serve.

———————— *SERVES 8* ————————

# Chocolate Cake

175 g (6 oz) Butter or Margarine
175 g (6 oz) Tate & Lyle Caster Sugar
3 Eggs, Beaten
30 ml (2 tbsp) Lyle's Golden Syrup
100 g (4 oz) Self Raising Flour
50 g (2 oz) Cocoa Powder
1 Quantity Chocolate Fudge Icing (See Page 94)

Grease two 18-cm (7-inch) sandwich tins and line the bases with greased greaseproof paper. Cream the fat and sugar until pale and fluffy. Add the egg a little at a time, beating well. Stir in the golden syrup. Gradually fold in the flour, followed by the cocoa. Place half the mixture in each tin.

Bake in the oven at 190°C (375°F) mark 5 for about 20 minutes, or until they are well risen and firm to the touch. Turn out and cool on a wire rack.

When the cakes are cool, sandwich with half the Chocolate fudge icing and swirl the remainder on top of the cake with a palette knife.

*———— SERVES 6–8 ————*

# Almond Gingerbread

50 g (2 oz) Flaked Almonds
350 g (12 oz) Plain Flour
15 g (½ oz) Ground Ginger
25 g (1 oz) Stem Ginger, Chopped
75 g (3 oz) Lard
75 g (3 oz) Tate & Lyle Light Brown Soft Sugar
350 g (12 oz) Lyle's Golden Syrup
1 Egg, Beaten
7.5 ml (1½ level tsp) Bicarbonate of Soda

Grease a 1.5-litre (2¾-pint) plain ring mould. Sprinkle the almonds over the base. Sift together the flour and ginger, and add the stem ginger.

Gently heat together the lard, sugar, syrup and 50 ml (2 fl oz) water, making sure it does not boil. Stir the liquid into the flour, add the egg and beat well. Dissolve the bicarbonate of soda in 50 ml (2 fl oz) water and stir into the mixture. Pour over the almonds in the prepared mould and bake in the oven at 170°C (325°F) mark 3 for about 50 minutes. Turn out and cool on a wire rack.

*———— SERVES 6–8 ————*

# PRUNE AND NUT TEABREAD

275 g (10 oz) SELF RAISING FLOUR
7.5 ml (1½ LEVEL TSP) GROUND CINNAMON
PINCH OF SALT
75 g (3 oz) BUTTER OR BLOCK MARGARINE
30 ml (2 TBSP) LYLE'S GOLDEN SYRUP
50 g (2 oz) TATE & LYLE DEMERARA SUGAR
1 EGG, BEATEN
100 ml (4 fl oz) MILK
50 g (2 oz) WALNUTS, CHOPPED
125 g (4 oz) PITTED TENDERISED PRUNES

Grease and line a 1.3-litre (2¼-pint) shallow loaf tin. In a bowl combine the flour, cinnamon and salt. Rub in the fat until the mixture resembles fine breadcrumbs. Stir in the syrup and sugar, and make a well in the centre. Add the egg and milk to form a smooth dough.

Using floured hands, shape the mixture into sixteen even-sized balls. Place eight in the base of the prepared tin. Sprinkle over half the nuts and snip over all the prune flesh. Place the remaining balls on top and sprinkle over the remaining nuts.

Bake in the oven at 190°C (375°F) mark 5 for about 50 minutes or until firm to the touch, covering lightly if necessary. Turn on to a wire rack to cool.

Wrap in foil and leave for 1 or 2 days before slicing and buttering.

*SERVES 6–8*

# FROSTED CARROT CAKE

*Illustrated facing page 65*

225 g (8 oz) SELF RAISING FLOUR
10 ml (2 LEVEL TSP) BAKING POWDER
10 ml (2 LEVEL TSP) GROUND CINNAMON
150 g (5 oz) TATE & LYLE LIGHT BROWN SOFT SUGAR
25 g (1 oz) BRAN BUDS
225 g (8 oz) CARROTS, PEELED AND GRATED
2 EGGS
30 ml (2 TBSP) LYLE'S GOLDEN SYRUP
150 ml (¼ PINT) VEGETABLE OIL
½ QUANTITY SEVEN MINUTE FROSTING (SEE PAGE 93)

Grease and base line a 20.5-cm (8-inch) round cake tin. Mix together the flour, baking powder, cinnamon, sugar, Bran Buds and carrot.

Beat together the eggs, syrup and oil. Stir into the dry ingredients, beating well. Spoon into the prepared tin.

Bake in the oven at 180°C (350°F) mark 4 for about 50 minutes. Turn out on to a wire rack to cool.

Make the Seven minute frosting. Swirl over the cake and leave until set.

——————— *SERVES 6–8* ———————

# RAISIN MALT LOAF

225 g (8 oz) PLAIN FLOUR
1.25 ml (¼ LEVEL TSP) SALT
30 ml (2 LEVEL TBSP) TATE & LYLE DARK BROWN SOFT SUGAR
5 ml (1 LEVEL TSP) BICARBONATE OF SODA
150 g (5 oz) SEEDLESS RAISINS
50 g (2 oz) LYLE'S GOLDEN SYRUP
30 ml (2 LEVEL TBSP) MALT
ABOUT 150 ml (¼ PINT) MILK

Grease and line a loaf tin measuring 21.5 × 11.5 cm (8½ × 4½ inches). Sift together the flour, salt, sugar and bicarbonate of soda and add the raisins. Place the syrup and malt in a saucepan with half the milk and heat gently until melted. Make a well in the centre of the dry ingredients, and pour in the syrup mixture. Mix well together, adding more milk to give a sticky, stiff consistency. Put into the tin and bake in the oven at 170°C (325°F) mark 3 for 1–1¼ hours. Turn out and cool on a wire rack. Foil wrap and eat after a day.

——————— *SERVES 6–8* ———————

# Parkin

225 g (8 oz) Plain Flour
10 ml (2 level tsp) Baking Powder
10 ml (2 level tsp) Ground Ginger
50 g (2 oz) Butter or Block Margarine
50 g (2 oz) Lard
225 g (8 oz) Medium Oatmeal
100 g (4 oz) Tate & Lyle Caster Sugar
175 g (6 oz) Lyle's Golden Syrup
175 g (6 oz) Lyle's Black Treacle
60 ml (4 tbsp) Milk

Grease and base line a tin measuring 25.5 × 20.5 × 4 cm (10 × 8 × 1½ inches). Sift together the flour, baking powder and ginger. Rub in the fats and add the oatmeal and sugar. Heat together the syrup and treacle until warm, make a well in the dry ingredients and stir in the syrup and treacle mixture, and the milk. Mix until smooth, then pour into the tin.

Bake in the oven at 180°C (350°F) mark 4 for 45–60 minutes. The mixture will shrink away from the sides of the tin and may dip slightly in the centre. Turn out and cool on a wire rack.

Keep for at least a week before eating and, if liked, serve sliced and buttered.

*SERVES 8*

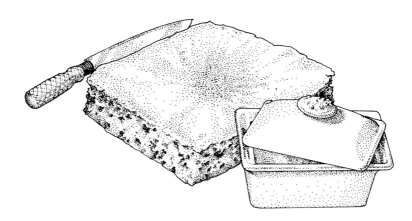

# DATE AND RAISIN TEABREAD

100 g (4 oz) BUTTER OR BLOCK MARGARINE
275 g (10 oz) PLAIN FLOUR, SIFTED
100 g (4 oz) STONED DATES, CHOPPED
50 g (2 oz) WALNUT HALVES, CHOPPED
100 g (4 oz) SEEDLESS RAISINS
100 g (4 oz) LYLE'S GOLDEN SYRUP
5 ml (1 LEVEL TSP) BAKING POWDER
5 ml (1 LEVEL TSP) BICARBONATE OF SODA
ABOUT 150 ml (¼ PINT) MILK

Grease and line a loaf tin measuring 25 × 15 cm (9¾ × 5¾ inches). Rub the fat into the flour and stir in the dates, walnuts, raisins and syrup. Mix the baking powder, bicarbonate of soda and milk and pour into the dry ingredients; mix to give a stiff dropping consistency.

Turn the mixture into the tin and bake in the oven at 170°C (325°F) mark 3 for about 30 minutes. Cover loosely with foil and cook for 45 minutes, until well risen and just firm to the touch. Turn out and cool on a wire rack.

———————— *SERVES 6–8* ————————

# MIXED FRUIT TEABREAD

175 g (6 oz) RAISINS
125 g (4 oz) SULTANAS
50 g (2 oz) CURRANTS
100 g (4 oz) TATE & LYLE LIGHT BROWN SOFT SUGAR
300 ml (½ PINT) COLD TEA
1 EGG, BEATEN
45 ml (3 TBSP) LYLE'S GOLDEN SYRUP
225 g (8 oz) PLAIN WHOLEMEAL FLOUR
7.5 ml (1½ LEVEL TSP) BAKING POWDER
2.5 ml (½ LEVEL TSP) MIXED SPICE

Grease and base line a 1.6-litre (2¾-pint) loaf tin. Soak the dried fruit and sugar in the tea overnight. Beat in the egg and syrup. Add the flour, baking powder and spice and mix well. Spoon into the prepared tin.

Bake in the oven at 170°C (325°F) mark 3 for 30 minutes. Cover loosely with foil and cook for 40–60 minutes until well risen and just firm. Turn on to a wire rack to cool. Wrap in foil, and eat after 1–2 days.

———————— *SERVES 8* ————————

# Uncooked Chocolate Cake

*Illustrated opposite*

175 g (6 oz) Digestive Biscuits, Crushed
25 g (1 oz) Walnuts, Coarsely Chopped
25 g (1 oz) Seedless Raisins
90 g (3½ oz) Butter or Margarine
25 g (1 oz) Tate & Lyle Caster Sugar
75 g (3 oz) Lyle's Golden Syrup
50 g (2 oz) Cocoa Powder

——— For the icing ———
50 g (2 oz) Plain Chocolate
15 ml (1 tbsp) Hot Water
65 g (2½ oz) Tate & Lyle Icing Sugar
Knob of Butter

Lightly grease a 19 or 20.5 cm (7½ or 8 inch) flan ring and place on a flat serving plate. Combine the biscuits with the walnuts and raisins. In a mixing bowl, cream the fat, sugar and syrup together until pale and fluffy. Sift and beat in the cocoa, then stir in the biscuit mixture. When the ingredients are well mixed, press evenly into the flan ring and chill for 8 hours or overnight.

To make the icing, break the chocolate into pieces and place in a small pan with the hot water. Sift in the icing sugar, add the butter and stir together over a very low heat until melted and blended. Leave to cool slightly.

Remove the flan ring and spread the chocolate icing over the cake. Leave in a cool place to set.

——— SERVES 8 ———

*Peanut and orange teabread; Uncooked chocolate cake.*
*Overleaf: Syrup teabread; Fruit crusted cider cake; Apple gingerbread ring.*

# GOLDEN SPONGE

175 g (6 oz) BUTTER OR MARGARINE
175 g (6 oz) TATE & LYLE CASTER SUGAR
30 ml (2 TBSP) LYLE'S GOLDEN SYRUP
3 EGGS, BEATEN
175 g (6 oz) SELF RAISING FLOUR
75 g (3 oz) WALNUTS, CHOPPED
TATE & LYLE ICING SUGAR TO DREDGE

——— *For the filling* ———
100 g (4 oz) BUTTER, SOFTENED
175 g (6 oz) TATE & LYLE ICING SUGAR
15 ml (1 TBSP) LYLE'S GOLDEN SYRUP
25 g (1 oz) WALNUTS, CHOPPED
GRATED RIND OF 1 LEMON
10 ml (2 TSP) LEMON JUICE

Grease and line two 20.5-cm (8-inch) sandwich tins. Cream the fat and sugar until light and fluffy. Beat in the syrup. Add the eggs a little at a time, beating thoroughly after each addition. Fold the flour into the sponge mixture. Stir in the nuts.

Turn into the prepared tins and bake in the oven at 190°C (375°F) mark 5 for 25–30 minutes or until well risen and golden. Turn out and leave to cool on a wire rack.

For the filling, cream the butter and icing sugar until smooth and fluffy. Add the syrup, nuts, lemon rind and juice, and mix well.

When the cakes are cold, sandwich together with the filling. Dust the surface of the cake with icing sugar.

——————— *SERVES 6–8* ———————

*Syrup chip cookies; Coffee sandwich creams; Gingernuts.*

# GINGER LOAF CAKE

175 g (6 oz) BUTTER OR MARGARINE
75 g (3 oz) TATE & LYLE DARK BROWN SOFT SUGAR
75 g (3 oz) LYLE'S GOLDEN SYRUP
3 EGGS
225 g (8 oz) SELF RAISING FLOUR
30–45 ml (2–3 LEVEL TBSP) GROUND GINGER
4 PIECES OF STEM GINGER, FINELY CHOPPED (OPTIONAL)
25 g (1 oz) FLAKED ALMONDS

Grease and base line a 23 × 12.9 cm (9 × 5 inch) loaf tin. Cream the butter, then add the sugar and syrup and continue creaming until the mixture is light and fluffy. Add the eggs, one at a time, beating well between each addition.

Sift together the flour and the ground ginger and fold into the creamed mixture. Fold in the chopped ginger (if used). Turn into the loaf tin. Sprinkle the flaked almonds over, press in lightly and bake in the oven at 180°C (350°F) mark 4 for about 1 hour 10 minutes until risen and firm to the touch.

*SERVES 8*

# LUSCIOUS CIDER CAKE

175 g (6 oz) BUTTER OR MARGARINE
175 g (6 oz) TATE & LYLE DARK BROWN SOFT SUGAR
3 EGGS
175 g (6 oz) SELF RAISING FLOUR
45–60 ml (3–4 TBSP) SWEET CIDER
300 ml (½ PINT) DOUBLE CREAM
15 ml (1 TBSP) LYLE'S GOLDEN SYRUP
25 g (1 oz) TATE & LYLE ICING SUGAR, SIFTED
15 g (½ oz) WALNUTS, ROUGHLY CHOPPED

Grease and line two 19-cm (7½-inch) sandwich tins. Cream together the fat and sugar until light and fluffy. Gradually beat in the eggs, one at a time. Mix in the flour and half the cider to form a soft dropping consistency. Divide the mixture between the prepared sandwich tins and smooth the top.

Bake in the oven at 190°C (375°F) mark 5 for 35 minutes. Cool on a wire rack. Whip the cream until thick and fold in the remaining cider, the syrup and the icing sugar. Spread half the cream filling over one half of the sponge and sandwich together. Spread the rest over the top, and sprinkle with nuts.

*SERVES 6–8*

# BISCUITS
# AND BUNS

## GINGERBREAD MEN

350 g (12 oz) PLAIN FLOUR
5 ml (1 LEVEL TSP) BICARBONATE OF SODA
10 ml (2 LEVEL TSP) GROUND GINGER
100 g (4 oz) BUTTER OR MARGARINE
175 g (6 oz) TATE & LYLE DARK BROWN SOFT SUGAR
60 ml (4 TBSP) LYLE'S GOLDEN SYRUP
1 EGG, BEATEN
CURRANTS TO DECORATE

Grease two baking sheets. Sift together the flour, bicarbonate of soda and ground ginger. Rub the fat into the sifted ingredients with the fingertips, add the sugar and mix well. Warm the syrup slightly and stir into the rubbed-in mixture, with the egg, to give a pliable dough.

Knead until smooth and roll out thinly on a floured work surface. Using a gingerbread man cutter, cut out the men until all the dough has been used. Carefully lift the men on to the prepared baking sheets, keeping them well apart. On to each man, put 3 currants for the eyes and mouth.

Bake in the oven at 190°C (375°F) mark 5 for 10–15 minutes or until evenly coloured. Cool on a wire rack.

*————— MAKES ABOUT 20—————*

## Syrup Oat Squares

100 g (4 oz) Self Raising Flour
100 g (4 oz) Rolled Oats
150 ml (¼ pint) Vegetable Oil
100 g (4 oz) Lyle's Golden Syrup
100 g (4 oz) Tate & Lyle Demerara Sugar
1 Egg
60 ml (4 tbsp) Milk

Lightly oil and base line a 19-cm (7½-inch) square tin. Put the flour and oats into a bowl. Gently warm the oil, syrup and sugar in a saucepan. Beat the egg with the milk. Make a well in the centre of the dry ingredients and pour the liquids into it. Beat well for 1–2 minutes.

Pour into the prepared tin and bake at 170°C (325°F) mark 3 for about 1 hour or until firm to the touch. Cool on a wire rack.

Store for a few days before cutting up into squares.

———— *MAKES 9*————

## Syrup Oat Scones

350 g (12 oz) Self Raising Flour
15 ml (3 level tsp) Baking Powder
5 ml (1 level tsp) Ground Ginger
75 g (3 oz) Butter or Block Margarine
50 g (2 oz) Porridge Oats
60 ml (4 tbsp) Lyle's Golden Syrup
About 200 ml (7 fl oz) Milk, at Room Temperature

Grease and preheat two baking sheets in the oven. Sift together the flour, baking powder and ground ginger into a bowl.

Rub in the fat until the mixture resembles fine breadcrumbs. Stir in the oats. Warm the syrup gently and add to the milk. Mix the dry ingredients to a soft dough with the syrup and milk, adding more milk if necessary.

Roll out to 1 cm (½ inch) thick on a floured work surface and cut into 5-cm (2-inch) triangles, kneading and re-rolling the dough. Place the scones on the prepared baking sheets. Brush with milk and bake in the oven at 230°C (450°F) mark 8 for 10–12 minutes or until risen and golden brown.

———— *MAKES ABOUT 20*————

# COFFEE SANDWICH CREAMS

*Illustrated facing page 73*

75 g (3 oz) BUTTER OR MARGARINE
75 g (3 oz) TATE & LYLE CASTER SUGAR
1 EGG, SEPARATED
15 ml (1 LEVEL TBSP) INSTANT COFFEE POWDER
ABOUT 30 ml (2 TBSP) MILK
200 g (7 oz) PLAIN FLOUR
12 WALNUT HALVES
30 ml (2 TBSP) LYLE'S GOLDEN SYRUP

Grease two baking sheets. Cream the fat and sugar together until pale and fluffy. Beat in the egg yolk. Dissolve the coffee powder in the milk and add to the creamed mixture. Add the flour and mix to a soft dough, adding a little more milk if necessary.

Roll out on a lightly floured work surface to about 1 cm (½ inch) thick. Cut into twenty-four rounds, using a 4-cm (1½-inch) cutter. Place on the prepared baking sheets, prick with a fork. Place the walnut halves on half of the biscuits.

Bake in the oven at 180°C (350°F) mark 4 for 10–15 minutes until light golden brown. Cool on a wire rack.

Meanwhile, prepare the filling. Whisk the egg white and 15 ml (1 tbsp) syrup together in a bowl over a pan of hot water until pale, fluffy and quite thick. Use the filling to sandwich the cold biscuits together in pairs, topping a plain biscuit with a walnut one. Warm the remaining syrup in a pan and use to glaze the walnuts.

———————— *MAKES 12* ————————

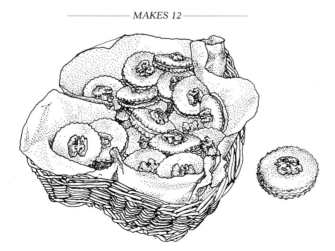

# Spiced Syrup Buns

100 g (4 oz) Butter or Margarine
45 ml (3 tbsp) Lyle's Golden Syrup
2 Eggs, Lightly Beaten
175 g (6 oz) Self Raising Flour
5 ml (1 level tsp) Ground Ginger
5 ml (1 level tsp) Ground Cinnamon
Grated Rind of 1 Orange
50 g (2 oz) Tate & Lyle Icing Sugar, Sifted
15 ml (1 tbsp) Orange Juice

Put twelve paper cases into patty tins. Cream the fat and syrup until fluffy. Beat in the eggs, and add the flour, spices and orange rind. Mix well.

Two-thirds fill the cases with the mixture and bake in the oven at 200°C (400°F) mark 6 for 15–20 minutes until golden. Cool on a wire rack.

When cold, beat the icing sugar with the orange juice until smooth. Coat the buns with the orange icing.

*——————— MAKES ABOUT 12 ———————*

# Cornish Fairings

100 g (4 oz) Plain Flour
Pinch of Salt
5 ml (1 level tsp) Baking Powder
5 ml (1 level tsp) Bicarbonate of Soda
5 ml (1 level tsp) Ground Ginger
2.5 ml (½ level tsp) Mixed Spice
50 g (2 oz) Butter or Block Margarine
50 g (2 oz) Tate & Lyle Caster Sugar
45 ml (3 tbsp) Lyle's Golden Syrup

Grease two baking sheets. Sift the flour with the salt, baking powder, bicarbonate of soda, ginger and mixed spice. Rub in the butter until the mixture resembles breadcrumbs and add the sugar. Warm the syrup and add it to the other ingredients; mix well to a fairly stiff consistency.

Roll into small balls and place them 10 cm (4 inches) apart on the prepared baking sheets. Bake in the oven at 200°C (400°F) mark 6 for about 8 minutes until golden brown. Cool on a wire rack.

*——————— MAKES 24 ———————*

# Ginger Biscuits

225 g (8 oz) Plain Flour
2.5 ml (½ level tsp) Bicarbonate of Soda
10 ml (2 level tsp) Ground Ginger
125 g (4 oz) Butter or Block Margarine
225 g (8 oz) Tate & Lyle Demerara Sugar
1 Egg, Beaten
15 ml (1 tbsp) Lyle's Golden Syrup

Grease two baking sheets. Sift together the flour, bicarbonate of soda and ginger and rub in the fat until the mixture resembles breadcrumbs. Stir in the sugar, breaking up any lumps. Make a well in the centre and put in the egg and golden syrup. Mix well and knead lightly to form a crumbly dough.

Roll the dough into small balls the size of walnuts. Place on the prepared sheets about 5 cm (2 inches) apart and press down lightly. Bake in the oven at 180°C (350°F) mark 4 for 15–20 minutes until golden. Leave on the sheets for a few minutes to let the biscuits crisp as they cool. Then transfer to wire racks and cool completely.

——————— *MAKES ABOUT 30* ———————

# Gingernuts

*Illustrated facing page 73*

100 g (4 oz) Self Raising Flour
2.5 ml (½ level tsp) Bicarbonate of Soda
5 ml (1 level tsp) Ground Ginger
5 ml (1 level tsp) Ground Cinnamon
10 ml (2 level tsp) Tate & Lyle Caster Sugar
50 g (2 oz) Butter or Margarine
75 g (3 oz) Lyle's Golden Syrup

Grease two baking sheets. Sift together the flour, bicarbonate of soda, ginger, cinnamon and sugar. Melt the fat in a saucepan and stir in the syrup. Stir this mixture into the dry ingredients and mix well.

Immediately roll the mixture into small balls, place well apart on the baking sheets and flatten slightly. Bake in the oven at 190°C (375°F) mark 5 for 15–20 minutes until golden. Cool for a few minutes before lifting carefully from the baking sheets on to a wire rack. Finish cooling, and store in an airtight tin.

——————— *MAKES ABOUT 24* ———————

## Coburg Buns

*Illustrated opposite*

12 Blanched Almonds
150 g (5 oz) Plain Flour
2.5 ml (½ level tsp) Bicarbonate of Soda
2.5 ml (½ level tsp) Ground Allspice
2.5 ml (½ level tsp) Ground Ginger
2.5 ml (½ level tsp) Ground Cinnamon
50 g (2 oz) Butter or Margarine
50 g (2 oz) Tate & Lyle Caster Sugar
1 Egg, Beaten
15 ml (1 tbsp) Lyle's Golden Syrup
60 ml (4 tbsp) Milk

Grease twelve fluted bun tins or put twelve paper cases into patty tins. Sift together the flour, bicarbonate of soda and spices. Cream the fat and sugar until pale and fluffy. Add the egg a little at a time, beating well after each addition.

Mix the syrup and milk and add to the creamed fat alternately with the flour mixture, folding in lightly with a metal spoon.

Divide the mixture between the tins and bake in the oven at 180°C (350°F) mark 4 for about 25 minutes or until firm to the touch. Turn out, decorate each bun with a whole almond, and leave to cool on a wire rack.

——————— *MAKES 12* ———————

## Butterscotch Bars

*Illustrated facing page 81*

75 g (3 oz) Butter or Margarine
75 g (3 oz) Lyle's Golden Syrup
100 g (4 oz) Stoned Dates, Chopped, or Seedless Raisins
50 g (2 oz) Glacé Cherries, Chopped
50 g (2 oz) Walnuts, Chopped
100 g (4 oz) Wheatmeal Biscuits, Crushed

Heat the fat and golden syrup in a saucepan. Bring to the boil, stirring continuously, and boil for 2–3 minutes. Set aside.

Mix together the remaining ingredients, then add the syrup mixture and stir until coated evenly. Press into an 18-cm (7-inch) square cake tin.

Chill in the refrigerator until set, then cut into twelve bars for serving.

——————— *MAKES 12* ———————

*Coburg buns; Mocha cup cakes.*

## Apricot Flapjacks

*Illustrated opposite*

50 g (2 oz) Dried Apricots
75 g (3 oz) Butter or Margarine
50 g (2 oz) Tate & Lyle Demerara Sugar
30 ml (2 tbsp) Lyle's Golden Syrup
175 g (6 oz) Rolled Oats

Grease a 20.5-cm (8-inch) round cake tin. Simmer the apricots gently in 150 ml (¼ pint) water for 10–15 minutes until softened. Place in a food processor or blender and liquidise to form a purée. Heat the fat, sugar and syrup together in a saucepan until melted. Pour on to the rolled oats and stir in the apricot purée. Mix well and spoon into the tin, pressing down well. Bake in the oven at 180°C (350°F) mark 4 for 40–45 minutes. Leave in the tin to cool, then cut into wedges.

——————— *MAKES 16–20* ———————

## Cinnamon Thins

50 g (2 oz) Butter or Margarine
15 ml (1 level tbsp) Tate & Lyle Caster Sugar
50 g (2 oz) Lyle's Golden Syrup
5 ml (1 level tsp) Ground Cinnamon
40 g (1½ oz) Plain Flour
40 g (1½ oz) Chopped Mixed Nuts

Line two baking sheets with non-stick paper or oiled foil. Over a very gentle heat, melt together the fat, sugar, golden syrup and ground cinnamon.

Off the heat, stir in the flour and nuts. Immediately place six spoonfuls of mixture on to each prepared baking sheet, leaving room for spreading. Spread each one out thinly with an oiled, round bladed knife to approximately 9 cm (3½ inches) diameter. Don't worry if holes appear in the rounds; these disappear on baking.

Bake the trays of biscuits in the oven in rotation at 200°C (400°F) mark 6 for 10–12 minutes or until a deep golden brown all over.

Carefully lift the biscuits with a fish slice and fold over a lightly oiled rolling pin or empty wine bottle to cool into a curled shape. Cool completely then ease off the pin.

Store in an airtight container and eat on day of making.

——————— *MAKES 12* ———————

*Apricot flapjacks; Butterscotch bars.*

# DATE AND SYRUP BARS

175 g (6 oz) DATES, STONED AND CHOPPED
45 ml (3 TBSP) LYLE'S GOLDEN SYRUP
30 ml (2 TBSP) LEMON JUICE
10 ml (2 LEVEL TSP) PLAIN FLOUR
125 g (4 oz) SELF RAISING FLOUR
125 g (4 oz) TATE & LYLE DEMERARA SUGAR
150 g (5 oz) ROLLED OATS
175 g (6 oz) BUTTER OR MARGARINE, MELTED

Grease and base line an 18-cm (7-inch) square tin, 2.5 cm (1 inch) deep. Place the dates in a saucepan with the syrup, strained lemon juice, plain flour and 120 ml (8 tbsp) water. Bring slowly to the boil, stirring, and cook gently for 3–4 minutes. Turn out and cool.

Mix the self raising flour, sugar, oats and melted fat together and spread half over the base of the tin, pressing down well. Spread the date mixture over the top, and finish with the remaining crumble mixture, pressing evenly all over the surface.

Bake in the oven at 190°C (375°F) mark 5 for about 25 minutes until golden; cool in the tin for at least 30 minutes. Cut into bars and ease out of the tin.

——————— *MAKES ABOUT 18* ———————

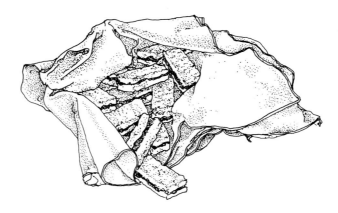

# Chocolate Raisin Squares

75 g (3 oz) Butter or Margarine
100 g (4 oz) Tate & Lyle Caster Sugar
2 Eggs
75 g (3 oz) Lyle's Golden Syrup
50 g (2 oz) Plain Chocolate, Melted
225 g (8 oz) Plain Flour
5 ml (1 level tsp) Bicarbonate of Soda
2.5 ml (½ level tsp) Cream of Tartar
30 ml (2 level tbsp) Cocoa Powder
30–45 ml (2–3 tbsp) Milk
100 g (4 oz) Raisins
50 g (2 oz) Walnut Pieces

——— *For the frosting* ———
100 g (4 oz) Butter or Margarine
250 g (9 oz) Tate & Lyle Icing Sugar, Sifted
50 g (2 oz) Plain Chocolate
15 ml (1 tbsp) Lyle's Golden Syrup

Grease and line a 28 × 18 × 4 cm (11 × 7 × 1½ inch) tin. Cream together the fat and sugar until light and fluffy. Beat in the eggs and then the syrup and melted chocolate, which should be cool but still liquid.

Sift the flour, bicarbonate of soda and cream of tartar into the mixture. Blend the cocoa to a paste with a little milk. Stir in and, when well blended, add the raisins and walnuts. Beat well.

Turn the mixture into the prepared tin, level and bake in the oven at 180°C (350°F) mark 4 for about 40 minutes or until risen and firm. Turn out and cool on a wire rack.

For the frosting, cream the fat until light and fluffy, then beat in the icing sugar. Break the chocolate into pieces and place with the syrup in a bowl over hot water to melt. Stir into the creamed mixture. Pour the frosting over the cake and swirl with a knife. When set, cut into squares.

——— *MAKES 16* ———

## CHOCOLATE CINNAMON SLICES

450 g (1 lb) PLAIN COOKING CHOCOLATE
225 g (8 oz) BUTTER OR MARGARINE
30 ml (2 TBSP) LYLE'S GOLDEN SYRUP
10 ml (2 LEVEL TSP) GROUND CINNAMON
2 EGGS
450 g (1 lb) DIGESTIVE BISCUITS, CRUSHED

Break the chocolate into pieces and place in a saucepan with the fat and syrup. Heat gently, stirring, until the chocolate has melted. Add the cinnamon and stir well together.

Remove from the heat and beat in the eggs. Stir the crushed biscuits into the chocolate mixture and mix well. Spoon into a 900-g (2-lb) loaf tin, and leave in the refrigerator overnight or until firm.

To serve, turn out and cut into slices.

———— *MAKES 20* ————

## CRISP OAT COOKIES

75 g (3 oz) PLAIN FLOUR
2.5 ml (½ LEVEL TSP) BICARBONATE OF SODA
75 g (3 oz) TATE & LYLE CASTER SUGAR
75 g (3 oz) ROLLED OATS
75 g (3 oz) BUTTER OR MARGARINE
15 ml (1 TBSP) MILK
15 ml (1 TBSP) LYLE'S GOLDEN SYRUP

Grease two baking sheets. Sift the flour and bicarbonate of soda together and stir in the sugar and oats. Heat the fat, milk and syrup together in a saucepan until melted, pour over the dry ingredients and mix well.

Roll into small balls and place 9 cm (4 inches) apart on the baking sheets. Flatten slightly and bake in the oven at 150°C (300°F) mark 2 for about 25–30 minutes or until firm. Cool on the sheets for 2–3 minutes before removing.

———— *MAKES 20* ————

# Chocolate Crackles

225 g (8 oz) Plain Chocolate
15 ml (1 tbsp) Lyle's Golden Syrup
50 g (2 oz) Butter or Margarine
50 g (2 oz) Cornflakes

Place twelve paper cases on a baking sheet. Break the chocolate into pieces, put in a saucepan with the golden syrup and fat and melt together over a low heat.

Remove the pan from the heat and stir in the cornflakes, mixing well. Divide the mixture equally between the paper cases and leave to set.

### VARIATIONS

1. Add some finely chopped nuts, glacé cherries, sultanas or dates and stir in with the cornflakes.

2. Melt some chocolate and drizzle over the top, or decorate each chocolate crackle with a glacé cherry.

———————— *MAKES 12* ————————

# Syrup Chip Cookies

*Illustrated facing page 73*

100 g (4 oz) Butter or Margarine
50 g (2 oz) Tate & Lyle Caster Sugar
175 g (6 oz) Lyle's Golden Syrup
1 Egg
2.5 ml (½ tsp) Vanilla Flavouring
175 g (6 oz) Self Raising Flour
1.25 ml (¼ level tsp) Salt
75 g (3 oz) Almonds, Chopped
75 g (3 oz) Chocolate Chips or Plain Chocolate, Chopped

Grease three baking sheets. Cream the fat, sugar and syrup until light and fluffy. Beat in the egg and vanilla flavouring. Sift the flour and salt together and lightly beat into the mixture. Fold in the nuts and chocolate.

Place in small spoonfuls on the baking sheets, allowing plenty of room to spread. Bake in the oven at 190°C (375°F) mark 5 for about 15 minutes or until golden brown. Allow to firm slightly before transferring to a wire rack to cool.

———————— *MAKES ABOUT 32* ————————

# WALNUT CRISPS

*Illustrated facing page 88*

50 g (2 oz) BUTTER OR MARGARINE
50 g (2 oz) TATE & LYLE CASTER SUGAR
30 ml (2 TBSP) LYLE'S GOLDEN SYRUP
25 g (1 oz) WALNUT PIECES, FINELY CHOPPED
25 g (1 oz) STEM GINGER, FINELY CHOPPED
50 g (2 oz) PLAIN FLOUR
2.5 ml (½ LEVEL TSP) GROUND GINGER

Line two or three baking sheets with non-stick paper. Warm the fat, sugar and syrup together in a saucepan until well blended then stir in the walnuts and stem ginger. Sift the flour and ground ginger together and stir into the mixture.

Place small spoonfuls of the mixture well apart on the prepared baking sheets. Bake the biscuits in the oven in rotation, at 180°C (350°F) mark 4 for 10 minutes or until golden brown.

Leave to firm up on the baking sheets for about 1 minute then ease off with a fish slice or palette knife and lay over a rolling pin to set into a curl.

After about 5 minutes when the biscuits are cool and crisp, ease off the rolling pin and, when quite cold, store in an airtight container.

———— *MAKES ABOUT 18* ————

# Rich Drop Scones

225 g (8 oz) Plain Flour
10 ml (2 level tsp) Cream of Tartar
5 ml (1 level tsp) Bicarbonate of Soda
5 ml (1 level tsp) Salt
10 ml (2 tsp) Lyle's Golden Syrup
10 ml (2 level tsp) Tate & Lyle Caster Sugar
1 Egg
About 300 ml (½ pint) Milk

Preheat a griddle. Sift together the dry ingredients. Add the syrup, sugar and egg and gradually beat in the milk to give a thick batter.

Spoon the mixture on to the griddle in small rounds. When bubbles start to burst and the undersides are golden, turn the scones over and cook on the second side; allow about 5 minutes altogether. Place the scones inside a clean tea towel over a wire cake rack.

Serve the scones while still fresh and warm, spread with butter.

——————— *MAKES ABOUT 24* ———————

# Chocolate Biscuit Bars

225 g (8 oz) Plain Chocolate
30 ml (2 tbsp) Lyle's Golden Syrup
225 g (8 oz) Butter or Margarine
60 ml (4 tbsp) Double Cream
225 g (8 oz) Digestive Biscuits, Crushed
50 g (2 oz) Raisins
50 g (2 oz) Glacé Cherries, Halved
50 g (2 oz) Flaked Almonds, Toasted

Grease a 20.5-cm (8-inch) square tin. Break the chocolate into pieces and place in a bowl over a pan of hot water. Add the golden syrup, fat and cream. When the chocolate and butter have melted, remove the pan from the heat and cool slightly. Mix the biscuits, fruit and nuts into the chocolate mixture.

Turn the mixture into the prepared tin, lightly level the top, then chill for at least 1 hour. Cut into bars before serving.

——————— *MAKES 12* ———————

# BRANDY SNAPS

*Illustrated opposite*

50 g (2 oz) LYLE'S GOLDEN SYRUP
50 g (2 oz) TATE & LYLE CASTER SUGAR
50 g (2 oz) BUTTER OR MARGARINE
50 g (2 oz) PLAIN FLOUR
2.5 ml (½ LEVEL TSP) GROUND GINGER
FINELY GRATED RIND OF ½ A LEMON
5 ml (1 TSP) BRANDY

——— *For the filling* ———
300 ml (½ PINT) DOUBLE CREAM
30 ml (6 TSP) BRANDY
15 ml (1 LEVEL TBSP) TATE & LYLE ICING SUGAR

Line three or four baking sheets with non-stick paper. Place the syrup, sugar and fat in a small heavy-based saucepan and warm gently until the sugar dissolves and the fat melts. Take the pan off the heat. Sift the flour and the ground ginger together, and stir into the syrup mixture together with the lemon rind and the brandy.

Using about 10 ml (2 tsp) of the mixture for each snap, spoon out on to the prepared sheets, allowing not more than four to a sheet to leave room for spreading. Bake in the oven at 180°C (350°F) mark 4 for 8–10 minutes, or until surfaces are bubbly and golden brown. Rotate the sheets or cook in two batches if necessary.

Leave the snaps to firm up *slightly* – about 1 minute – then roll loosely around the greased handles of wooden spoons. Leave to set on a wire rack then ease out the spoons.

For the filling, whip the cream until stiff, then whip in the brandy and icing sugar. Spoon into a piping bag fitted with a 5 mm (¼ inch) star vegetable nozzle. Pipe the cream into either end of the snaps and pile up on a dish. Leave in a cool place for 2 hours before serving.

——— *MAKES ABOUT 14* ———

*Brandy snaps; Walnut crisps.*
*Overleaf: Fruit punch; Apple cider cup; Hawaiian quencher.*

# Mocha Cup Cakes

*Illustrated facing page 80*

30 ml (2 TBSP) COFFEE ESSENCE
75 g (3 oz) BUTTER OR MARGARINE
75 g (3 oz) TATE & LYLE CASTER SUGAR
15 ml (1 TBSP) LYLE'S GOLDEN SYRUP
225 g (8 oz) PLAIN FLOUR
30 ml (2 LEVEL TBSP) COCOA POWDER
5 ml (1 LEVEL TSP) BICARBONATE OF SODA
45 ml (3 TBSP) MILK
2.5 ml (½ TSP) VANILLA FLAVOURING
CHOCOLATE CURLS TO DECORATE (OPTIONAL)

———— *For the icing* ————
75 g (3 oz) PLAIN CHOCOLATE
40 g (1½ oz) BUTTER
300 g (11 oz) TATE & LYLE ICING SUGAR

Put twenty paper cases (base size 5 cm/2 inches) into patty tins. In a large saucepan, gently heat together the coffee essence, 200 ml (7 fl oz) water, the fat, sugar and syrup, stirring until the sugar dissolves. Bring to the boil and simmer for 5 minutes. Leave until cool.

Sift the flour and cocoa together into the cool mixture. Dissolve the bicarbonate of soda in the milk and the vanilla flavouring and add to the mixture. Beat until smooth.

Spoon the chocolate mixture into the paper cases and bake in the oven at 180°C (350°F) mark 4 for 15–20 minutes or until risen and firm to the touch. Cool on a wire rack.

For the icing, break up the chocolate and melt with the butter and 60 ml (4 tbsp) water in a bowl over hot water. Sift in the icing sugar and beat until smooth. Keep the icing liquid over the hot water, adding a little more water if necessary, beating it if it begins to set. Put a large spoonful of icing on each cake, tipping to reach the edges. Leave to set then decorate with chocolate curls.

———————— *MAKES ABOUT 20* ————————

*Green tomato and onion pickle; Apple ginger jam; Pickled pears with kumquats; Syrup lemon curd.*

# SAUCES
# AND
# FROSTINGS

## Walnut Rum Sauce

175 g (6 oz) Tate & Lyle Dark Brown Soft Sugar
10 ml (2 level tsp) Instant Coffee Powder
90 ml (6 tbsp) Single Cream or Evaporated Milk
25 g (1 oz) Butter or Margarine
15 ml (1 tbsp) Lyle's Golden Syrup
15 ml (1 tbsp) Rum
50 g (2 oz) Walnuts, Roughly Chopped

Combine in a saucepan the sugar, coffee, cream or evaporated milk, fat and golden syrup. Cook over a low heat to dissolve the sugar, bring to the boil and boil gently, stirring, for 2–3 minutes, or until thickened. Stir in the rum and the chopped walnuts.

Serve walnut rum sauce either cold or warm, with vanilla ice cream. This sauce may also be bottled and stored for a short time.

——————— *MAKES ABOUT 450 ml (¾ PINT)* ———————

# Chocolate Fudge Sauce

*Illustrated between pages 56 and 57*

75 ml (5 TBSP) SINGLE CREAM
25 g (1 oz) COCOA POWDER
125 g (4 oz) TATE & LYLE CASTER SUGAR
175 g (6 oz) LYLE'S GOLDEN SYRUP
25 g (1 oz) BUTTER OR MARGARINE
PINCH OF SALT
2.5 ml (½ TSP) VANILLA FLAVOURING

Combine all the ingredients except the vanilla flavouring in a saucepan over low heat and mix well. Slowly bring to the boil, stirring occasionally. Boil for 5 minutes, then add the vanilla flavouring.

Cool the sauce slightly before serving. Use with ice cream, profiteroles and other desserts.

*————— MAKES ABOUT 450 ml (¾ PINT) —————*

# Fudge Sauce

50 g (2 oz) PLAIN CHOCOLATE
25 g (1 oz) BUTTER OR MARGARINE
60 ml (4 TBSP) WARM MILK
225 g (8 oz) TATE & LYLE LIGHT BROWN SOFT SUGAR
30 ml (2 TBSP) LYLE'S GOLDEN SYRUP
5 ml (1 TSP) VANILLA FLAVOURING

Break up the chocolate and put into a bowl standing over a saucepan of hot water. Add the fat and leave until the chocolate and fat have melted, stirring once or twice. Blend in the milk and transfer the chocolate mixture to a saucepan. Add the sugar and golden syrup. Stir over a low heat until the sugar has dissolved. Bring to the boil and boil steadily without stirring for 5 minutes.

Remove the pan from the heat. Add the vanilla flavouring and mix well. Serve hot with ice cream or steamed baked puddings.

*————— MAKES ABOUT 450 ml (¾ PINT) —————*

# TOFFEE SAUCE

*Illustrated facing page 56*

50 g (2 oz) TATE & LYLE CASTER SUGAR
125 g (4 oz) BUTTER OR MARGARINE
150 ml (¼ PINT) DOUBLE CREAM
50 g (2 oz) LYLE'S GOLDEN SYRUP
VANILLA FLAVOURING

Place the sugar, fat, cream and golden syrup in a bowl, and add vanilla flavouring to taste. Stand over a saucepan of water and heat gently. Stir until the butter has melted and the ingredients are well mixed. Serve hot.

——————— *MAKES ABOUT 300 ml (½ pint)* ———————

# SYRUP SAUCE

60 ml (4 TBSP) LYLE'S GOLDEN SYRUP
JUICE OF ½ A LEMON

Warm the syrup with 45 ml (3 tbsp) water in a saucepan, stir well and simmer, uncovered, for 2–3 minutes; add the lemon juice. Serve syrup sauce hot with steamed or baked sponge puddings.

——————— *MAKES ABOUT 150 ml (¼ PINT)* ———————

# BUTTERSCOTCH SAUCE

25 g (1 oz) BUTTER OR MARGARINE
30 ml (2 LEVEL TBSP) TATE & LYLE LIGHT BROWN SOFT SUGAR
15 ml (1 TBSP) LYLE'S GOLDEN SYRUP
45 ml (3 LEVEL TBSP) CHOPPED NUTS
LEMON JUICE (OPTIONAL)

Warm the fat, sugar and syrup in a saucepan until well blended. Boil for 1 minute and stir in the nuts and lemon juice, if using, to taste. Serve the sauce at once, with vanilla or coffee ice cream.

——————— *MAKES ABOUT 100 ml (4 fl oz)* ———————

# Butterscotch Nut Sauce

10 ml (2 level tsp) Custard Powder
15 ml (1 tbsp) Lyle's Golden Syrup
15 ml (1 level tbsp) Tate & Lyle Dark Brown Soft Sugar
15 g (½ oz) Butter or Margarine
Few Drops of Lemon Flavouring
30 ml (2 level tbsp) Chopped Nuts

**B**lend the custard powder with 150 ml (¼ pint) water. Put the syrup, sugar and fat in a saucepan and heat gently until melted. Remove from the heat and mix in the custard powder mixture. Bring to the boil, stirring, and mix in a little lemon flavouring and the nuts.

Serve the sauce either hot or cold, with baked or steamed puddings.

*————— MAKES ABOUT 150 ml (¼ PINT) —————*

# Seven Minute Frosting

1 Egg White
175 g (6 oz) Tate & Lyle Caster Sugar
Pinch of Salt
Pinch of Cream of Tartar
30 ml (2 tbsp) Lyle's Golden Syrup

**P**ut all the ingredients except the golden syrup into a bowl with 30 ml (2 tbsp) water and whisk lightly. Place the bowl over a pan of hot water and heat, whisking continuously, until the mixture thickens sufficiently to stand in peaks. This will take about 7 minutes, depending on the whisk used and the heat of the water. Stir in the syrup.

Pour the frosting over the top of the cake and spread with a palette knife. Eat the cake on the day of frosting.

*Note*:
The quantities given make sufficient frosting
to cover an 18-cm (7-inch) cake. To cover the top and sides of a
three or four layer cake, double the quantities.

*————— MAKES ABOUT 175 g (6 oz) —————*

# Fudge Icing

225 g (8 oz) Tate & Lyle Icing Sugar
30 ml (2 tbsp) Lyle's Golden Syrup
45 ml (3 tbsp) Milk
75 g (3 oz) Butter or Margarine
5 ml (1 tsp) Vanilla Flavouring

Sift the icing sugar into a mixing bowl. Put the remaining ingredients in a saucepan and stir over a low heat until the fat is melted and the mixture is almost boiling. Pour at once into the sifted icing sugar and stir with a wooden spoon until smooth.

*For a coating icing*: pour over the prepared cake as soon as the icing is thick enough to coat the back of the spoon generously.

*For a roughed-up icing*: leave the mixed icing to cool a little then stir gently until thick enough to leave a trail. Spread over the prepared cake and rough-up with the tip of a knife.

*For a fluffier roughed-up icing or for a filling cream*: allow the mixed icing to cool, then beat briskly with a wooden spoon until the icing is the consistency of buttercream. Spread over the cake. For a softer filling cream, beat a little extra fat into the mixture before using.

*For piping*: put a little of the mixed icing into a piping bag with the required piping nozzle and leave to cool until the icing is thick enough to hold its shape. This will give a glossy, piped decoration which will be the same colour as the smooth coating icing.

Leftover fudge icing can always be used to flavour buttercream fillings, or it can be melted down again in a basin over a saucepan of simmering water until the flowing consistency is restored, and then used for smooth coating or piping.

## VARIATIONS

*Chocolate fudge icing*: Add 15 ml (1 level tbsp) cocoa powder sifted in with the icing sugar.

*Coffee fudge icing*: Add 10 ml (2 tsp) coffee essence to the contents of the saucepan.

———————— *MAKES ABOUT 300 g (11 oz)* ————————

# SWEETS

## Peppermint Humbugs

*These popular sweets are hard to make on your own,
so enlist the help of a friend. If liked, all of the toffee mixture can
be pulled to make humbugs without stripes.*

450 g (1 lb) Tate & Lyle Caster Sugar
1.25 ml (¼ level tsp) Cream of Tartar
15 ml (1 tbsp) Lyle's Golden Syrup
Few Drops of Peppermint Flavouring
Few Drops of Brown Food Colouring

Oil a marble or enamel slab or wooden chopping board. Dissolve the sugar in 150 ml (¼ pint) water in a large heavy-based saucepan. Mix the cream of tartar with 15 ml (1 tbsp) water and add to the saucepan with the golden syrup. Bring the mixture gently to 154°C (310°F) (hard crack stage), when a little of the syrup dropped into cold water separates into brittle threads. Pour the syrup on to the slab and allow to cool a little.

Using oiled palette knives, fold the sides of the toffee into the centre and add a few drops of peppermint flavouring. When the mixture is cool enough to handle, cut off one-third and pull this until it is pale in colour, but still soft.

Meanwhile your helper should add a few drops of food colouring to the remaining toffee and gently form into a thick roll. Divide the pulled toffee into four ropes and press these against the sides of the thick darker rope. Pull out gently to the required thickness and twist. The larger the size of humbug you want, the thicker you will need to make the roll. Using oiled scissors, cut into humbugs or cushions.

———————— *MAKES ABOUT 450 g (1 lb)*————————

## Plain Lollipops

*Illustrated opposite*

225 g (8 oz) Tate & Lyle Caster Sugar
100 g (4 oz) Lyle's Golden Syrup
Lollipop Sticks

Oil a marble or enamel surface. In a heavy-based saucepan, gently heat the sugar and syrup with 150 ml (¼ pint) water until the sugar has dissolved. Bring to the boil and boil to 130°C (265°F) (hard ball stage), when a little of the syrup dropped into cold water forms a ball which holds its shape when it is removed from the water.

Using a dessertspoon, pour a little of the syrup on to the oiled surface so that it forms rounds. Put a lollipop stick into each round while it is still soft, then pour on a little more syrup to cover the stick. Leave the lollipops to set hard, then carefully lift them from the slab and wrap them in cellophane.

———————— MAKES 18 ————————

## Lollipop Surprises

*Illustrated opposite*

175 g (6 oz) Lyle's Golden Syrup
Juice of 1 Lemon
Few Drops of Red Food Colouring (Optional)
About 30 Glacé Cherries, Washed and Thoroughly Dried
Lollipop Sticks

Boil the syrup and the lemon juice to 130°C (265°F) (hard ball stage), when a little of the syrup dropped into cold water forms a ball which holds its shape on removal from the water. Remove from the heat and add a few drops of colouring if liked. Put a whole cherry on a stick and dip it into the syrup, then twirl round to coat the fruit thoroughly. Lay the lollipop on a greased baking sheet to harden and repeat with the remaining mixture. Leave the lollipops to set hard, then wrap in cellophane.

———————— MAKES ABOUT 30 ————————

VARIATIONS
Replace the cherries with stoned dates or figs.

*Toffee apples; Plain lollipops; Lollipop surprises.*

## CHOCOLATE CARAMELS

25 g (1 oz) BUTTER OR MARGARINE
150 ml (¼ PINT) CONDENSED MILK
225 g (8 oz) TATE & LYLE CASTER SUGAR
120 ml (8 TBSP) LYLE'S GOLDEN SYRUP
50 g (2 oz) COCOA POWDER
2.5 ml (½ TSP) VANILLA FLAVOURING
225 g (8 oz) PLAIN CHOCOLATE, MELTED (OPTIONAL)

Grease an 18 × 12.5 cm (7 × 5 inch) tin. Melt the fat in a heavy-based saucepan and add the milk, sugar and syrup. Stir over a gentle heat until the sugar is dissolved. Bring to boiling point, add the cocoa and boil to 124°C (255°F) (hard ball stage), when a little of the syrup dropped into cold water forms a ball which holds it shape on removal from the water. Add the flavouring, pour the mixture into the tin and mark into pieces before completely set. Once the caramels are set, they may if liked be dipped into plain chocolate.

*———— MAKES ABOUT 450 g (1 lb)————*

## REFRIGERATOR FRUIT CARAMELS

*Illustrated opposite*

100 g (4 oz) STONED DATES, CHOPPED
100 g (4 oz) FIGS, CHOPPED
175 g (6 oz) SEEDLESS RAISINS
175 g (6 oz) CANDIED LEMON OR ORANGE PEEL, CHOPPED
100 g (4 oz) SHELLED NUTS, CHOPPED
15 ml (1 TBSP) LEMON JUICE
10 ml (2 TSP) LYLE'S GOLDEN SYRUP
DESICCATED COCONUT TO COAT

Grease a 20.5 × 15 cm (8 × 6 inch) tin. Mix all the fruits and nuts together and add the lemon juice and the golden syrup. Pack into the tin and leave in the refrigerator for several hours. Cut into small squares and roll these in the desiccated coconut. Place in paper cases.

*———— MAKES ABOUT 700 g (1½ lb)————*

*Creamy fudge; Chocolate fudge; Refrigerator fruit caramels.*

## ALMOND TOFFEE

450 g (1 lb) TATE & LYLE DEMERARA SUGAR
25 g (1 oz) BUTTER OR MARGARINE
2.5 ml (½ LEVEL TSP) CREAM OF TARTAR
2–3 DROPS OF ACETIC ACID
30 ml (2 TBSP) LYLE'S GOLDEN SYRUP
75 g (3 oz) BLANCHED ALMONDS, CHOPPED

Oil a marble or enamel slab or wooden chopping board. Dissolve the sugar in 150 ml (¼ pint) water in a heavy-based pan, cover and bring to the boil. Add the fat, cream of tartar, acetic acid and golden syrup. Cover again and boil for a few minutes.

Remove the lid and heat to 149°C (300°F) (hard crack stage), when a little of the syrup dropped into cold water separates into brittle threads. Pour on to the prepared surface, sprinkle with the nuts, and turn the sides to the middle using a greased palette knife. When cold enough to handle, pull the toffee lightly with oiled fingers. When nearly set, cut into cushions or squares. Wrap in waxed paper or cellophane when cold and store in an airtight tin.

*MAKES ABOUT 550 g (1¼ lb)*

## GOLDEN TOFFEE

450 g (1 lb) TATE & LYLE CASTER SUGAR
50 g (2 oz) BUTTER OR MARGARINE
10 ml (2 TSP) WHITE WINE VINEGAR
ABOUT 225 g (8 oz) LYLE'S GOLDEN SYRUP

Grease a 20.5 × 15 cm (8 × 6 inch) tin. Put all the ingredients with 15 ml (1 tbsp) water in a heavy-based saucepan and boil quickly to 149°C (300°F) (hard crack stage), when a little of the syrup dropped into cold water separates into brittle threads. Pour into the prepared tin and allow to cool. Mark the toffee into squares when it is almost set.

*MAKES ABOUT 700 g (1½ lb)*

# Chocolate Fudge

*Illustrated facing page 97*

450 g (1 lb) Tate & Lyle Caster Sugar
150 ml (¼ pint) Milk
150 g (5 oz) Butter or Margarine
100 g (4 oz) Plain Chocolate
50 g (2 oz) Lyle's Golden Syrup

Grease a 20.5 × 15 cm (8 × 6 inch) tin. Place all the ingredients in a heavy-based saucepan. Stir over a low heat until dissolved. Bring to the boil and boil gently for about 10 minutes to 116°C (240°F) (soft ball stage), when a little of the syrup dropped into cold water forms a soft ball which flattens on removal from the water. Remove from the heat, stand the pan on a cool surface for 5 minutes, then beat until thick and beginning to grain. Pour into the prepared tin and mark into squares. Cut when cold and store in an airtight container.

### VARIATION
*Fruit and nut fudge*: Add 50 g (2 oz) chopped nuts and 50 g (2 oz) seedless raisins to the mixture before beating.

——————— *MAKES ABOUT 700 g (1½ lb)* ———————

# CREAMY FUDGE

*Illustrated facing page 97*

450 g (1 lb) TATE & LYLE LIGHT BROWN SOFT SUGAR
150 ml (¼ PINT) MILK
15 ml (1 TBSP) LYLE'S GOLDEN SYRUP
50 g (2 oz) BUTTER OR MARGARINE
196-g (6.91-oz) CAN CONDENSED MILK

Grease an 18 × 12.5 cm (7 × 5 inch) tin. In a heavy-based saucepan, dissolve the sugar in the milk over a gentle heat, then add the syrup and fat. Bring to the boil and boil for 2–3 minutes before stirring in the condensed milk. Re-boil and heat to 116°C (240°F) (soft ball stage), when a little of the syrup dropped into cold water forms a soft ball which flattens on removal from the water. Beat until thick and beginning to grain, then pour into the tin. Mark the fudge into squares and leave until set.

——————— *MAKES ABOUT 700 g (1½ lb)* ———————

# TOFFEE APPLES

*Illustrated facing page 96*

450 g (1 lb) TATE & LYLE DEMERARA SUGAR
50 g (2 oz) BUTTER OR MARGARINE
10 ml (2 TSP) WHITE WINE VINEGAR
15 ml (1 TBSP) LYLE'S GOLDEN SYRUP
6–8 MEDIUM APPLES
WOODEN STICKS

Heat the sugar, fat, vinegar and syrup gently with 150 ml (¼ pint) water in a heavy-based saucepan. When the sugar has dissolved, boil rapidly for 5 minutes until it reaches 143°C (290°F) (soft crack stage), when a little of the syrup dropped into cold water separates into hard but not brittle threads.

Wipe the apples and push the sticks into the cores. Dip the apples into the toffee, twirl around for a few seconds to allow excess toffee to drip off, then leave to cool and set on a greased baking sheet or waxed paper.

The toffee apples should be eaten on the day they have been made.

——————— *MAKES ABOUT 7* ———————

# Toffee Humbugs

450 g (1 lb) Tate & Lyle Light Brown Soft Sugar
50 g (2 oz) Butter or Margarine
30 ml (2 tbsp) Lyle's Golden Syrup
2.5 ml (½ level tsp) Cream of Tartar
Few Drops of Vanilla or Almond Flavouring, or 2.5 ml
(½ level tsp) Ground Ginger, Cinnamon or Cloves to Flavour

Oil a marble or enamel slab or wooden chopping board. Put everything except the cream of tartar and flavouring in a large heavy-based saucepan with 150 ml (¼ pint) water. Dissolve the sugar and bring to the boil. Add the cream of tartar and boil to 143°C (290°F) (soft crack stage), when a little of the syrup dropped into cold water separates into hard but not brittle threads. Add the flavouring and pour the mixture on to the prepared surface.

Leave the toffee until a skin has formed, then, using a flexible greased palette knife, turn the edges into the centre, continuing to work the toffee until it is cool and firm enough to handle. Scrape the toffee off the slab, form it into a rope and pull.

Quickly shape the toffee into a rope about 2 cm (¾ inch) in diameter, and with oiled scissors cut off 2-cm (¾-inch) pieces, half twisting the toffee rope each time to give the correct humbug shape. Wrap each piece in waxed or cellophane paper and store the toffee in an airtight tin.

*————— MAKES ABOUT 450 g (1 lb) —————*

# Treacle Toffee

450 g (1 lb) Tate & Lyle Demerara Sugar
1.25 ml (¼ level tsp) Cream of Tartar
75 g (3 oz) Butter or Margarine
100 g (4 oz) Lyle's Black Treacle
100 g (4 oz) Lyle's Golden Syrup

Grease a 30.5 × 10 cm (12 × 4 inch) tin. Dissolve the sugar in 150 ml (¼ pint) water in a large heavy-based saucepan over a low heat. Add the remaining ingredients and bring to the boil. Boil to 132°C (270°F) (soft crack stage), when a little of the syrup dropped into cold water separates into hard but not brittle threads. Pour into the tin, cool for 5 minutes, then mark into squares and leave to set.

*————— MAKES ABOUT 800 g (1¾ lb) —————*

# Almond Brittle

350 g (12 oz) Tate & Lyle Preserving Sugar
225 g (8 oz) Lyle's Golden Syrup
10 ml (2 level tsp) Powdered Glucose
25 g (1 oz) Butter or Margarine
75 g (3 oz) Blanched Almonds, Chopped and Toasted
2.5 ml (½ tsp) Lemon Flavouring
7.5 ml (1½ level tsp) Bicarbonate of Soda

Oil a marble or enamel slab or wooden chopping board. Dissolve the sugar in 150 ml (¼ pint) water with the golden syrup and the glucose, stirring occasionally. Boil to 149°C (300°F) (hard crack stage), when a little of the syrup dropped into cold water separates into brittle threads. Add the fat, almonds and flavouring and reheat to melt the fat.

Stir in the bicarbonate of soda and pour in a very thin sheet on to the prepared surface. Roll out immediately with an oiled rolling pin and break up when firm and brittle.

*————— MAKES ABOUT 700 g (1½ lb) —————*

# PRESERVES

## Apple Ginger Jam

*Illustrated facing page 89*

2 kg (4 lb) Cooking Apples
225 g (8 oz) Preserved Ginger, Drained and Chopped
45 ml (3 tbsp) Lyle's Golden Syrup
Grated Rind and Juice of 3 Lemons
1.5 kg (3 lb) Tate & Lyle Preserving Sugar

Peel, core and slice the apples. Place the cores and peel on a piece of muslin and tie up to make a bag. Put the apples and bag in a preserving pan with 900 ml (1½ pints) water, and simmer gently until the fruit is pulpy. Remove the muslin bag and mash the apples or rub them through a nylon sieve.

Return the apple purée to the pan and add the ginger, golden syrup, the rind and juice of the lemons and the sugar. Bring to the boil, stirring constantly, and boil rapidly for 10 minutes to 105°C (221°F) or setting point. If you have no sugar thermometer test that the jam has reached setting point by spooning a little on to a chilled saucer. Leave it to cool then push a finger across the surface. When setting point has been reached, the surface will wrinkle.

Take the pan off the heat and remove any scum with a slotted spoon. Leave the jam to stand for 15 minutes before pouring into preheated jars. Place a disc of waxed paper across the surface of the jam, and cover the jar with damped cellophane, secured with an elastic band.

——————— *MAKES 2.75–3.5 kg (5½–7 lb)* ———————

# GREEN TOMATO AND ONION PICKLE

*Illustrated facing page 89*

2 kg (4 lb) GREEN TOMATOES, SLICED
750 g (1½ lb) LARGE ONIONS, SKINNED AND SLICED
75 ml (5 LEVEL TBSP) SALT
2.4 LITRES (4 PINTS) MALT VINEGAR
150 ml (¼ PINT) LYLE'S GOLDEN SYRUP
15 ml (1 LEVEL TBSP) MUSTARD POWDER
10 ml (2 LEVEL TSP) CURRY POWDER
1.25 ml (¼ LEVEL TSP) CAYENNE PEPPER
5 ml (1 LEVEL TSP) MIXED SPICE

Layer the tomato and onion slices in a bowl, sprinkling each layer liberally with the salt, and leave for 24 hours.

Drain and rinse the tomatoes and onions well. Put the vinegar, syrup and spices into a saucepan and bring to the boil. Add the vegetables and cook very gently for 5 minutes. Pour into preheated jars and cover at once with airtight, vinegar-proof tops.

———— *MAKES ABOUT 2.8 kg (6 lb)* ————

# PICKLED PEARS WITH KUMQUATS

*Illustrated facing page 89*

15 ml (1 LEVEL TBSP) CORIANDER SEEDS
PIECE OF CINNAMON STICK ABOUT 5 cm (2 INCHES) LONG
300 ml (½ PINT) WHITE WINE VINEGAR
175 g (6 oz) TATE & LYLE CASTER SUGAR
60 ml (4 TBSP) LYLE'S GOLDEN SYRUP
225 g (8 oz) KUMQUATS
450 g (1 lb) COOKING PEARS, PEELED, CORED AND QUARTERED

Tie the coriander seeds and cinnamon in a muslin bag. Place in a medium saucepan with the vinegar, sugar and syrup and heat gently until the sugar dissolves. Bring the syrup to the boil, strain, then add the kumquats and simmer, covered, for 20 minutes. Add the pears and cook gently for a further 5 minutes or until the fruit is barely tender.

Lift the fruit out of the pan and pack into preheated jars. Boil down the syrup to thicken a little then pour over the fruit. Cover at once with airtight, vinegar-proof lids.

———— *MAKES ABOUT 900 g (2 lb)* ————

# Date and Orange Chutney

450 g (1 lb) Oranges
450 g (1 lb) Onions, Skinned
750 g (1½ lb) Dates, Stoned
225 g (8 oz) Sultanas
750 g (1½ lb) Tate & Lyle Preserving Sugar
100 g (4 oz) Lyle's Golden Syrup
30 ml (2 level tbsp) Salt
1.25 ml (¼ level tsp) Cayenne Pepper
1.5 litres (2½ pints) Malt Vinegar

Finely grate the rind of the oranges. Peel off the pith and slice the oranges, discarding the pips. Mince together the oranges, onions, dates and sultanas. Place the sugar, syrup, salt, cayenne and vinegar in a large saucepan. Heat gently, stirring, until the sugar has dissolved, then bring to the boil and add the minced fruits and half the orange rind.

Simmer gently, stirring occasionally, for about 1 hour until no excess liquid remains and the mixture is thick. Stir in the remaining orange rind.

Spoon the chutney into preheated jars and cover immediately with airtight and vinegar-proof tops.

*MAKES ABOUT 2 kg (4 lb)*

# Lemon and Apple Chutney

2 Lemons, Washed
300 ml (½ pint) Cider Vinegar
90 ml (6 tbsp) Lyle's Golden Syrup
225 g (8 oz) Tate & Lyle Preserving Sugar
2.5 ml (½ level tsp) Ground Ginger
225 g (8 oz) Cooking Apples, Peeled, Cored and Sliced
1 Medium Onion, Skinned and Finely Chopped
25 g (1 oz) Sultanas

Halve the lemons lengthways and slice thinly, discarding any pips. Put the lemon slices in a saucepan with sufficient water to cover and simmer gently for 45 minutes until tender. Remove the lemon slices from the pan with a slotted spoon. Stir the vinegar, syrup, sugar and ginger into the pan juices and heat gently, stirring continuously, until the sugar has dissolved.

Add the apples to the liquid with the onion, sultanas and cooked lemon. Bring to the boil and simmer gently, uncovered, for 20–25 minutes, stirring occasionally, until the onion is soft and no excess liquid remains.

Spoon the chutney into preheated jars and cover at once with airtight, vinegar-proof tops.

*MAKES ABOUT 1 kg (2 lb)*

# Orange and Lemon Pickle

4 Medium Oranges, Washed
1 Lemon, Washed
300 ml (½ pint) Distilled Vinegar
125 g (4 oz) Lyle's Golden Syrup
125 g (4 oz) Tate & Lyle Caster Sugar
Piece of Cinnamon Stick About 5 cm (2 inches) Long
8 Cloves
10 ml (2 level tsp) Coriander Seeds

Thinly slice the oranges, halve each slice crosswise and remove the pips. Slice the lemon, discard pips and chop finely. Place the fruit in a saucepan, cover with cold water, bring to the boil, cover and simmer for about 1 hour or until the fruit and peel are tender. Drain off the liquid through a nylon sieve.

Place the vinegar and remaining ingredients in a saucepan and warm gently until the sugar has dissolved; simmer for 10 minutes. Strain the mixture and return to the pan with the fruit. Boil gently, uncovered, for 15 minutes or until nearly all the liquid has evaporated and the fruit is of a pulpy consistency.

Pour into preheated jars and cover at once with airtight, vinegar-proof tops.

*MAKES ABOUT 1 kg (2 lb)*

# Syrup Lemon Curd

*Illustrated facing page 89*

3 Egg Yolks
45 ml (3 tbsp) Lyle's Golden Syrup
Finely Grated Rind and Juice of 1 Lemon
50 g (2 oz) Unsalted Butter, Softened

Place the egg yolks, syrup, lemon rind and 60 ml (4 tbsp) strained lemon juice in a double boiler or small bowl placed over a pan of simmering water. Beat well with a wooden spoon to mix.

Cook slowly over a gentle heat, stirring all the time and gradually beating in the butter. Cook until the mixture thickens slightly; it can take as long as 15 minutes. Do not over-heat or the mixture will curdle.

Pour into preheated jars and cover with cellophane secured with an elastic band. When cold, store in the refrigerator for 3–4 weeks. Serve the syrup lemon curd spread over hot toast or scones.

*MAKES ABOUT 225 g (8 oz)*

# DRINKS

## Still Lemonade

3 Lemons
45 ml (3 tbsp) Lyle's Golden Syrup
90 ml (1½ pints) Boiling Water

Wash the lemons and peel off the rind thinly with a potato peeler. Put the rind and syrup into a basin or large jug and pour on the boiling water. Cover and leave to cool, stirring occasionally. Add the juice of the lemons and strain the lemonade. Serve chilled.

———— *MAKES ABOUT 1.1 LITRES (2 pints)* ————

## Hawaiian Quencher

*Illustrated between pages 88 and 89*

150 ml (¼ pint) Natural Yogurt
300 ml (½ pint) Pineapple Juice
10 ml (2 tsp) Lyle's Golden Syrup
1 Egg White, Lightly Beaten
15 g (½ oz) Desiccated Coconut, Toasted
Glacé Cherries and Pineapple Cubes to Garnish

Whisk the yogurt, pineapple juice and syrup together until blended. Dip the rims of two large tumblers in the egg white and then into the toasted coconut. Serve garnished with the fruit.

———— *SERVES 2* ————

# Fruit Punch

*Illustrated between pages 88 and 89*

60 ml (4 TBSP) LYLE'S GOLDEN SYRUP
300 ml (½ PINT) ORANGE JUICE
150 ml (¼ PINT) LEMON JUICE
300 ml (½ PINT) GRAPEFRUIT JUICE
ORANGE SLICES TO DECORATE

Combine the syrup with the fruit juices and 300 ml (½ pint) water and chill. Serve in tall glasses decorated with orange slices.

——————— *MAKES ABOUT 1.1 LITRES (2 pints)* ———————

# Fruit Flip

10 ml (2 TSP) LYLE'S GOLDEN SYRUP
JUICE OF 1 ORANGE
JUICE OF 1 LEMON
1 EGG YOLK
15 ml (1 TBSP) SHERRY

Mix the syrup, orange and lemon juice, egg yolk and sherry together and whisk for about 1 minute. Serve at once in a tall glass.

——————— *SERVES 1* ———————

# Banana Milk Shake

568 ml (1 PINT) MILK
1 BANANA, PEELED AND THINLY SLICED
10 ml (2 TBSP) LYLE'S GOLDEN SYRUP
A DASH OF LEMON JUICE
30 ml (2 TBSP) VANILLA ICE CREAM

Put all the ingredients except the ice cream into an electric blender and blend for 30–60 seconds until frothy. Serve immediately in tall glasses topped with the vanilla ice cream.

——————— *SERVES 2* ———————

# Apple Cider Cup

*Illustrated between pages 88 and 89*

2 Eating Apples, Peeled, Cored and Sliced
Thinly Pared Rind and Juice of 1 Lemon
8 Cloves
30 ml (2 tbsp) Lyle's Golden Syrup
1 Litre (2 pints) Dry Cider
300 ml (½ pint) Soda Water

Put the apples into a bowl with the lemon juice and rind and the cloves. Place the syrup in a saucepan with about 300 ml (½ pint) cider, and bring to the boil. Pour over the ingredients in the bowl and leave to cool. When cold, add the rest of the cider and the soda water. Strain and serve the cider cup garnished with the apple slices.

———— *MAKES ABOUT 1.7 LITRES (3 pints)* ————

# MULLED ALE

1 LEMON
1.1 LITRES (2 PINTS) ALE
150 ml (¼ PINT) RUM
30 ml (2 TBSP) LYLE'S GOLDEN SYRUP
PINCH OF NUTMEG
PINCH OF CINNAMON
PINCH OF GROUND CLOVES

Slice the lemon and discard the pips. Pour the ale, rum and 600 ml (1 pint) water into a large saucepan. Add the syrup and spices and heat gently until the syrup melts. Continue heating until the mixture is almost boiling. Serve hot with lemon slices floating in the liquid.

*MAKES ABOUT 1.7 LITRES (3 pints)*

# SPICY PUNCH

*Illustrated on the jacket*

600 ml (1 PINT) ORANGE JUICE
300 ml (½ PINT) PINEAPPLE JUICE
GRATED RIND AND JUICE OF 1 LEMON
2.5 ml (½ LEVEL TBSP) GROUND NUTMEG
2.5 ml (½ LEVEL TBSP) GROUND MIXED SPICE
6 CLOVES
45 ml (3 TBSP) LYLE'S GOLDEN SYRUP
1 LITRE (2 PINTS) GINGER ALE, CHILLED
CRUSHED ICE

Mix the fruit juices, lemon rind, spices and syrup in a large jug with 600 ml (1 pint) water. Chill. Strain the liquid and add the ginger ale and some crushed ice before serving.

*MAKES ABOUT 2.8 LITRES (5 pints)*